Unconditional Remembrance

Your Connection to Source

Laurie Seymour

Scribe Hive Publishing

Pueblo, Colorado

The Baca Institute
Denver, Colorado 80203
laurie@thebacainstitute.com

Unconditional Remembrance: Your Connection to Source — 1st edition

ISBN Paperback: 978-1-962112-27-7
ISBN eBook: 978-1-962112-28-4

Published through Scribe Hive Publishing LLC
Pueblo, Colorado

www.scribehivepublishing.com
A women-owned publishing cooperative driven to share great stories that want to be told.

Editor: Lois Rose

Cover Design: Cathi Stephenson, Book Cover Express

Cover Image: Passage to the Light, an intuitive flow painting by Annet Hoeijmans-Boon

Interior Design: Gwen Gades, Be a Purple Penguin

Publisher's Note

The material in this book is intended for educational purposes only. It is sold with the understanding that neither the author nor the publisher is engaged in rendering medical or any other professional services or prescribing any technique as a form of treatment for physical, emotional, or medical problems. While the publisher and author have used their best efforts in preparing this book, they make no representations or warranties with respect to the accuracy or completeness of the contents of this book and specifically disclaim any implied warranties of merchantability or fitness for a particular purpose. The advice and strategies contained herein may not be suitable for your situation. You should consult with a professional when appropriate. Neither the publisher nor the author shall be liable for any loss of profit or any other commercial damages, including but not limited to special, incidental, consequential, personal, or other damages.

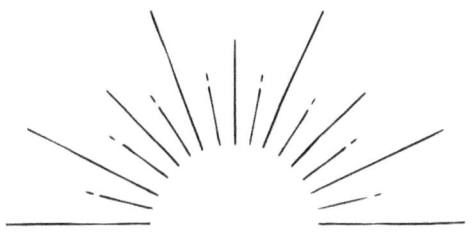

Dedication

For all those who are listening for their inner
voice, and who long to remember...

For Dawn, my incredible daughter, who stirs me to be who I am,
and for Henry and William, my grandsons who bring such light.

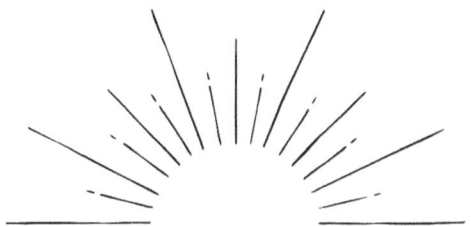

Table of Contents

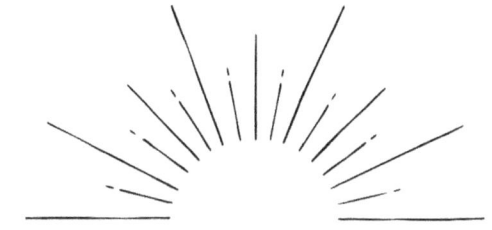

Foreword

Note: This is a foreword unlike most others you have read. Usually, the foreword is reserved for someone well-known, who is chosen to add credibility to what you are about to read. You likely don't know Dawn Taylor, who wrote this and who passed in 2008. I met Dawn in 1987, and she was the most impactful person in my life. In 1984, Dawn was initiated as a Reiki Master into the lineage of Dr. Mikao Usui. In 1985, in Koyasan, Japan, she was initiated into the lineage of Kobo Daishi. In 1991, in Lourdes, France, she was initiated into the lineage of the Essenes. Dawn is the reason I am writing this book. She opened my heart to the universal truth of our original connection with Source. Crista Marie Miller brought through this message from her.

Dawn's Message

When I first met Laurie, I could see the searching in her eyes, always questioning, always putting the puzzle pieces together in a way that not many did. She was a profound student, and I was very deeply honored to teach her from my own initiations that came through my Higher Self and Source.

During one of my initiations, I was shown the unique way in which humanity interacts. I had always been fascinated by how human nature came into existence. When I was a little girl, I heard a fable about a little boy who swallowed the universe. I would envision in my backyard or riding my bike that the universe was inside me. I knew it, I could feel it!

I also began to witness it within everyone else. It made me sad that this knowledge was invisible to most. I knew, at such a young age, with every bit of my soul, that it was my purpose to teach others about their Divine Right. So dear soul, know that the universe is within you. Yes, I am in the Spirit world, so I can now state this as an ultimate fact.

Laurie drew my attention over time. She had a presence about her that was curious and yet solid in who she was, even at the times when she did not consciously know it. Sure, we all question who we are from time to time, but she had a surety deep within her that I admired. I knew she would develop into an amazing mentor.

It is my hope that I taught Laurie to trust her own instincts. To recognize the inner knowing that is our eternal compass. She is a natural teacher and leader. Knowing that she would be a guide to many, she armed herself with tools of knowledge, energy components, and fortitude. Please know that as you read this, you have the same built-in guidance system, that when honed, will never steer you in the wrong.

I try to teach all my new students that disconnection from Source is not a punishment. It is a learning opportunity for soul growth. I know that wanting to be connected to something bigger, bolder, brighter is a longing that every human desires. I hope that you will find comfort as you read *Unconditional Remembrance*.

Through our connection, I helped Laurie write this book. I told her that she must write this story, to share in the teachings. She balked at first, but I knew this would become a reality.

This book is a testament to anyone who wants to expand their own self-knowing. Having the pleasure of being a mentor to Laurie and now reviewing her life here on the other side has allowed me to understand the path she has taken. She went into the field of psychology to learn about the inner workings of the human experience that always fascinated her. She knew she was going to be able to guide many and help heal them while holding space for them to discover themselves as well. The inner knowing path is sacred to behold. Laurie has that unique frequency to hold space while others discover the radiant energy within themselves. We all have that light within us. It is our job to turn it on.

Please know that when an energy is not in alignment with you, it will vibrate away from you. Pay attention to circumstances and people that this occurs with. It is our job within the human body to recognize what is for us, and what is not. I am thankful to say that I mastered this. It was all about listening to the inner voice.

One of the greatest choices of incarnating into the human experience is to experience love in all dimensions. I knew that I held within me the Divine Love of Source. Some would call it "Christ Consciousness," some would call it Source, some would call it the Holy Spirit...It has many names. I only knew that it was Pure Love. I followed my own truth, my own calling, my own passion in order to enlighten others. I know if you are reading these words, you have a calling to do that as well.

Now, I must emphasize that every single one of you has this gift. It was my mission on earth to show others their own spark within themselves. I hope I did justice for Laurie and the many others that I touched. I'm so incredibly grateful for this opportunity to open this book for you. To open your heart, soul, and mind into the words that Laurie will share. Her story is unique, but I know it will resonate with the multitude. So, sit back, let your wings spread open, and receive.

Dawn Taylor with Crista Marie Miller, May 2025

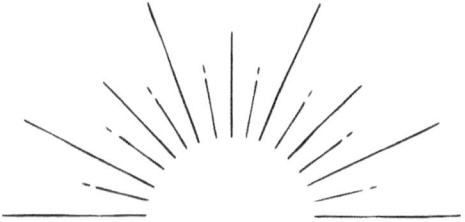

Preface

What if you knew, in every breath you took, that you were loved?

Our life experiences are not arbitrary. Nor are they ordained. They have meaning. It is up to us to make the journey of our own life as well as to give it meaning, so that we can remember the truth of who we are. Then we can once again know our connection to Source.

Growing up I felt like I was missing something that other people had. I didn't really know what it was—just that they had what I did not. This feeling mostly sat in the background, but it impacted the way I felt about myself and how I understood the world.

It guided my choices in ways that I could only see when I looked back on my life.

I lost my father before I was seven years old. So, in fact, I was different than the other kids in the neighborhood. But that's not what this feeling was about.

It was about losing the feeling of being loved so abruptly that I "forgot" what I was born knowing—that I came from love and was always loved. I became separated from myself. I forgot my connection with Source.

When I remembered and reclaimed this connection, each step of my life revealed new meaning. What I now understand is that without losing the feeling of being loved early in my life, I would never have gone looking for myself.

Perhaps if I could have seen how my own life was guiding me, I wouldn't have struggled so much. I wouldn't have steeped myself in self-doubt. I wouldn't have felt so alone.

I might have listened inside more closely.

But I would never have gone looking for myself. I had to want that more than anything else.

I chose psychology so that I could figure myself out.

I left a marriage.

I left the career I thought would explain me to myself.

In order to step into my purpose for being here, to be a way shower, I had to learn first to trust what was inside me.

I became a searcher. I had to keep searching until the search completed in me. I went beyond what I thought was wrong with me so that I could come back to who I am and have always been: an expression of Source.

It's not the details of my life that matter. But I will share parts of my journey so you have a context for the greater teaching you will discover here.

You will get to know Dawn. My experiences with her were the portal to a quantum leap in the arc of my life. It was the place of my re-discovery.

I know I'm not the only one who has felt different, as though I were in a life that did not fit me. One way I know is because I've had hundreds of clients and students who have shared their life journey with me. Over the years, they have given voice to profound changes as they allowed themselves to surrender to the strength within them. This *Unconditional Remembrance* of their connection with Source established a fundamental inner resource and support that is accessible in any moment. Inner guidance that they can trust from Source. Creative expression, inspiration to craft new solutions, products, and businesses.

Here is some of their feedback:

"I was reminded, again, that I'm not alone. I'm not doing this by myself."

"I can reconnect with myself with a breath."

"I am receiving more deeply than ever before."

"I feel spacious. I am nourished."

"I received a whole new course to offer with all of the components."

"I know how to get the answers to my own questions. I know I can trust the answers that come."

"Discernment. I am more aware now of when I agree or disagree with what comes to me."

"I have new confidence in my own powerful inner guidance."

"I am in flow with the Divine calling on my life every day."

"My whole life has changed. My business is thriving."

"I am filled with loving and activating energies to help generate the newness in my life."

"I feel a sense of calm and joy like never before."

"My connection with the Divine—and myself—is more grounded, steady, and strong."

"A new trust in life is anchored within me that has freed me to pursue my dreams in a big way."

Do you ever find yourself wondering how you got to where you are today, to this moment in your life?

You may not have had a parent who died when you were young, as I did. You may not have had people who didn't see who you are. You may not have forgotten your own truth.

Or you might have.

Know that you can unearth deeper value and meaning in your own life experiences. This book is your opportunity to recognize and acknowledge something that you've felt but haven't yet been able to name.

Let it be an invitation to *receive* your original blessing, your connection to Source. If you feel a resonance as you read, it can be a portal for you into the experience.

May you be inspired to experience *Unconditional Remembrance* and answer the call to be who you are.

This will change *your* world, and it will change *the* world. Because as each one of us remembers, the light expands. This collective force of Love takes us beyond any imagined separation from others.

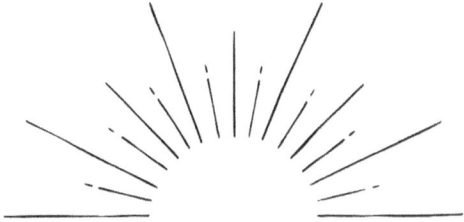

Note to the Reader

Through the adventure that you are about to embark upon, you will see how I came to know my own inner connection, a connection with Source, a Remembrance of the connection that is the Alpha and the Omega. It is my hope and desire that through this, you discover your own path of remembering your original connection, and that you feel the shift that transforms your everyday life into a lived blessing. Throughout the course of writing this book, just as I have been doing consistently in my life since 1987, I have tapped into the inner voice—my inner knowing that is directly connected with Source. The truth I knew as a young girl, and didn't know how I knew, came fully into being through the process of inner dialogue. It is this developing relationship that I hope you will witness so that you can recognize your own truth.

I say all this so that you can see this inner dialogue I share here is written from the perspective of guidance that was in answer to my questions. It is said *to* me, rather than *from* me. I have always found it helpful to receive guidance as a dialogue. You can find a whole list of questions to help you begin when you are ready for your own inner inquiry by visiting https:// bit.ly/4eWeOLi.

I also want to point out to you how I use the words *self* and *Self*. They are not interchangeable. I use the small "s" self when I am speaking about the personal, or individual self. The ego, the personality, and how you interact with the world are all contained in this. The expanded Self is sometimes called the Higher Self, sometimes the soul. It is that which is beyond the physical body and carries the connection with Universal Consciousness.

I want to suggest that this is not a book to read cover to cover in one sitting. I encourage you to keep it on your bedside table. Savor it as an invitation to explore your own journey of Remembrance. You can read a chapter, close the book, and let what you have read simmer in you. Let yourself find illumination wherever and however it comes.

Someone asked me recently how a book can give you an experience of your connection to Source. After all, it's not the information that ignites *Unconditional Remembrance*. Information is not inner knowing. This already lives in your cells. The connection must be awakened. This is part of the journey!

So, bring all of yourself as you read: your intuitive senses, curiosity, ideas, thoughts, and emotions. Pay attention to how you feel. Notice when you feel a resonance with the words. They may remind you of something that you once knew but forgot as life intervened. The forgetting isn't important. It is *remembering* that is necessary.

Go deeper. Find the place of connection within yourself and know it to be true. Anchor there. Ground in the light, this place of reception that lives within you. Become the witness and the experiencer at the same time.

As you anchor in Remembrance, you anchor light in the world.

In the first few years of The Baca Institute (then known as The Baca Journey), I wrote a weekly Friday Focus blog post that ended with this direction. You might use this process at the end of each chapter.

Take a breath. Release it. Take another. Devote some dedicated time of concentration/meditation. It doesn't need to be hours of quiet—perhaps only 15 minutes. Then allow this to simmer within you. Let your response bubble up into your awareness. Notice new ways of thinking, of images or ideas that arise spontaneously. Pay attention to your dreams.

Let it happen. Be aware. See where it leads you next. Let yourself savor this process of receiving from yourself. Don't judge whatever comes up, just receive it. Make notes. You may want to share something from this process. Sharing is an important way to anchor an insight in your body. It leads you to deeper insight. It stimulates action.

If you haven't read the Preface (and many people don't, because, of course, the book is calling!), I invite you to read it now. It's an important part of understanding the ground from which this book emerged.

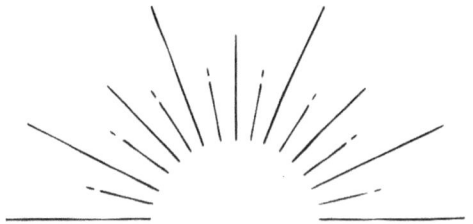

Principles from *Unconditional Remembrance*: Your Connection to Source

1. **Universal Connection:** Each person is an expression of the creative life force of the Universe, with an original, inherent connection to Source—a fundamental aspect of their being that is always present, even if forgotten.

2. **self vs. Self:** There is a distinction between self (ego/personality) and Self (expanded/Higher Self); Self carries the connection with the universal.

3. **Unconditional Love:** Unconditional love is your birthright. It is your original blessing. It is transformative both personally and collectively.

4. **Rediscovery Through Experience:** Life experiences, including feelings of separation or loss, serve as catalysts to rediscover and remember this connection to Source.

5. **Everything Is Energy:** The cells of the body are both receivers and transmitters. As the cells receive higher frequencies of energy, which are essentially encoded activators, higher levels of consciousness are made accessible.

6. **Embodiment of Love:** Experiencing love as a tangible, embodied vibration helps dissolve the sense of separation and loss, allowing you to remember your original connection to Source and to yourself.

7. **Inner Resource:** This embodied experience provides a constant inner resource and support, accessible at any moment, which brings a sense of calm, joy, and nourishment.

8. **Inner Law:** Life is designed to work. Inner Law is about how life works. Your awareness of how Inner Law works and your willingness to embrace it determines your experience of life.

9. **Trusted Guidance:** Inner guidance is available from Source and can be trusted. You cultivate this relationship through Inner Research that leads to discernment, confidence, and inspiration.

10. **Flow of Life:** In recognizing and releasing personal will in favor of surrendered will, you align with the greater flow of life and the wisdom of Source.

11. **Ongoing Remembrance:** The process of *Unconditional Remembrance* is ongoing and requires openness, commitment to inquire within, willingness to receive, and courage to act on inner guidance.

12. **Collective Impact:** As you awaken to your purpose, you contribute to a greater force of love and positive change in the world, reflecting the collective dimension of spiritual awakening.

As you remember and embody this connection, you contribute to a collective force of Love that can transform the world. Collective co-creation and the evolution of consciousness are possible when you remember and act from your connection to Source. This grows community, strengthens communication, and spurs innovation and creative solution building.

The Opening

Without the work I did with my vocal teacher Gene Worth, I would never have resonated with what I read on a flyer that arrived in the mail about an event the next week. Gene, who had been a performing singer for years, was then using vocal exercises to clear the body of old patterns. She focused on sound, vibration, and energy. We would sit at her kitchen table talking about life, before moving to the piano.

The event on the flyer was at a home in Lake Oswego, Oregon, just outside of Portland where I was living. I had been working as a therapist for about ten years. I had clients that evening and was loathe to cancel them. In fact, I had decided that I would not be able to go.

But I held on to the flyer.

Sid, my husband, had some chiropractic patients that night so it was clear he would not attend. Then my clients cancelled, and I had the opening to go. I asked my dearest friend, Jane, if she wanted to go join me. She was afraid it would be weird: that it would be filled with people that were from a religious sect or some kind of cult. I convinced her to go, saying we could always leave and get a cappuccino.

With the deal struck we went to this event. The room was full. There were no other places to sit, only spaces on the floor. By the time we all settled in, there was no place for even one other person.

Dawn entered the room. She wove her way through the people sitting on the floor, her soft presence impacting me as she passed. She was stunning, dressed in purples and mauves that set off her dark wavy hair; her dress flowed around her as she made her way to where the host stood waiting to introduce her. There was nothing remotely cultish about her, as Jane had feared.

She was lit from within.

I couldn't take my eyes off her. She was accompanied by four or five people. One of them, Patricia, spoke about her life and how it had transformed through her work with Dawn. Next, Richard spoke. His words were filled with an energy that felt unknown and unfamiliar. I didn't really understand them, yet still they resonated in me.

Then Dawn spoke. She was filled with such love that I could not do anything but be with her. My heart (was it that?) expanded in my chest. I felt energy moving through me. There was something here that I had not experienced before. All I knew was that I was drawn to this woman who *radiated*. Yes, that was the word; she radiated. She was indeed lit from within, and her words brought that feeling to me as well.

Dawn went around the room touching each of us on our chest and forehead. The room was silent, each person receiving the energy that she was transmitting.

Jane and I went to speak with her afterwards. We were equally electrified. I told Dawn how moved I was by the experience. What I said wasn't really important; I simply wanted a moment with her. And we learned there was to be an event that weekend.

When Jane and I had lunch the next day, the only topic of conversation was, of course, *what was it that we had just experienced? Would we go to the upcoming class?*

Yes, of course, we would. Jane was always one to leap into things. Me, not always so much. Perhaps it was her readiness to go without any hesitation. But I think there was a knowing within me that was not to be ignored, and that, of course, I would go! Sid decided to go, too, after hearing what happened for us.

The three of us went to a private home where the weekend class was to be held.

And, what a weekend that was! I experienced the "being" of Dawn, and the vibration of love and truth that she embodied.

The Original Separation

I invite you to consider that there is a time of existence before we are born. The memory of this lives in every cell of the body. Some of us have conscious memories of this—a kind of time between lives, if you will. The essence of this time is a feeling of oneness with all there is. There is a knowingness where separation simply doesn't exist.

As Michael Newton, Ph.D. says in *Journey of Souls*, "All souls are part of the same divine essence generated from one oversoul. This intelligent energy is universal in scope and so *we all share divine status.*"[1]

I see this as our original blessing; our essence is connection.

Then we are born! Our piece of the expression of the creative life force has to separate from this divine essence in order to "do" life. And so, this is what I conceive of as an *original separation.*

It doesn't mean that we actually are separate.

It's that we forget Source. We forget where we came from. Forgetting seems to be built into the "plan." It takes a kind of amnesia of our true nature to undertake the tasks that come before us in life. Whatever the learning that is ours to do in this lifetime is played out in the life we create.

We have this feeling of being separate only because we forget that we are actually connected, always and forever. Indeed, *nothing* separates us from our connection with Source. We *are* Source.

But in coming into the physical world, in believing that

---

1 Michael Newton, Ph.D., *Journey of Souls*, Llewellyn Press, 2023, p. 122

physical life is all there is, then *that* is all we see. We do not acknowledge or recognize the timeless nature of existence.

This is where love comes in, reminding us of the truth of our original blessing.

Loss

It was a few weeks before my seventh birthday. My brother was five. We were sitting on my bed with my mother. I heard my mother's voice as if from far, far away, and she was telling us that my father died the night before. Bobby began to laugh. It is the most powerful part of my memory. He was just young enough for death to be an unknown idea, so I imagine he didn't understand the meaning of my mother's words. Maybe he thought it was a joke. I remember crying, but I cannot feel myself back then. I see it like I'm watching a movie. We weren't allowed to go to the funeral, Bobby and me. They decided we were too young.

Of course, nobody ever asked us if we wanted to go.

So, I never got to say goodbye. I never got to see him in the casket—to see what "dead" looked like and to feel, however it felt to me. That missing piece hounded me for years, never allowing me to feel any closure. I didn't even believe he had died! I always imagined that he would someday reappear. Or that I would at long last find him.

But something occurs to me as I write these words. Closure was not what I needed. Connection was what I craved. My connection to him and through him to knowing that I was loved. It was the experience of being special, feeling loved, feeling unique—these were what I longed for almost every day.

The duality of my life—the split or separation, of self from Self—began in not allowing myself to remain connected with my father's love. With his death when I was not even seven years old, I was unable to keep alive the feeling of love.

There was nobody that stepped into that void.

Where was my mother? Stunned by his loss. Overwhelmed with the daily reality of four kids and no income and no life insurance. No time to breathe. She felt abandoned by my father! I was too young to know how she was before his death, but looking back, I am certain that then she just shut down. Survival became her focus. We were taken care of, but I wasn't cuddled. She didn't delight in me in a way that would have filled my being. *She* couldn't feel love, so I couldn't feel it from her. I longed for some sign from her. It never came, so I gave up.

So, if love wasn't in my environment to experience, then in my little girl self, it meant that love didn't exist.

What nonsense! I know that now. But back then, I learned instead the ways of the outer world, with its rules that did nothing to satisfy the yearning of that little girl's heart. I became smart and skilled at reading others so I could know what they wanted from me, aware of the changes in those around me so I could adjust as needed. It's the reason that when people got quiet and pulled back, I would immediately imagine they were judging me. I calibrated my actions for who and what was around me. What I sensed as a lack of presence from someone disturbed me. I was stuck in focusing outward.

I pulled away from the real truth: my connection with myself.

I recognize the pathway that I carved so long ago: one that took me all around the outer, physical world, experience by experience. Today, I realize that could only have taken me so far. But having barred the door to my inner world—where, of course, I would have felt that love that I longed to feel—I had no place to recover what I thought I had lost.

So it was that I journeyed far away from the source of that love. From Source. I spent years thinking I would find my father, imagining that he had not really and truly died. I think somewhere in me I still feel that. The little girl who longs to have her father come home and see his eyes light up, ready to hug his "Princess." What is revealing itself to me now is that while I was looking for him, it was in all the wrong places.

4

Call to My Father

Daddy, you are here now to tell me that you love me, that you always have and always will. But you went away, and I couldn't feel you. I didn't know where you had gone. I was bereft and oh so alone.

Your love was why I came here, what drew me to this family and this place in time.

And now, here you are, telling me that you have always been present and never really did leave.

What happened?

I closed the channels that would have allowed me to continue to feel my father. Why would I do that? What was it that turned me to look for truth outside of me, instead of remaining connected with myself and the Remembrance of where I came from?

That would certainly be my choice now. But I didn't feel safe doing that then. I felt alone, strange to myself, and abandoned. I became watchful: distrustful of the outside world, trying always to understand what was happening around me so that I could anticipate what was coming and protect myself.

In understanding, I thought, lay safety.

You are here now, and I so want to feel you. You must show me; and I must allow it. This is the space and time for me to discover you. I was going to say it's time for us to reconnect with each other. But you didn't leave me, except in the physical world. And, of course, that was where I was focused. Nobody told me that I could remain connected with you.

That's the thing. That was the truth, the message, the guidance that I needed, and I had nobody to provide it. The result was that I grew up not feeling loved and not knowing that that was even possible.

A Shadow of Remembrance

Mrs. Jacobson was my second-grade teacher at Feltonville Elementary in Philadelphia. She was young and fun. She would even visit the kids in the neighborhood.

One night I had a dream where I was a teacher in a school. I don't remember any of the details now, only that the dream really impacted me. When I went to school that morning, I told Mrs. Jacobson about the dream.

She asked me if I wanted to teach the class that day! Her idea was for me to give the class one of our timed arithmetic tests. Not exactly what I had in mind, but I was certainly game since I didn't really have anything!

She had me take the test ahead of time to ensure that I could do the work I was testing the class in. Arithmetic was already an area where I could flounder, especially with the pressure of being timed. But I made it through my own test and stood ready to take up my mantle.

There are two things that stand out to me now. One is the feeling of "rightness" when I was in front of the class. I felt like I was doing what I was supposed to do, and that I knew *what* to do. And that's the other thing. Everyone in the class simply accepted that I was doing this. I wasn't questioned or teased.

I knew without knowing how I knew. Over and over again in my life I have simply known things. As a young therapist in training, I would give feedback to clients in private sessions, or in workshops, with a deep sense of inner knowing of its truth. Yet because I was young and didn't have a lot of life experience, I was often accused of being cocky. And that I was speaking from book learning instead of my own life.

I didn't understand how I knew these things and couldn't line up my experience with any outside learning. So, I didn't know how to orient myself around it. There was nobody in my life who acknowledged my way of "knowing."

And with these experiences as a young therapist, the message was, "You have no way to know these things from your own experience. Don't be so smart."

That was true. I didn't have experiences to support what I knew from this lifetime.

However, those comments and judgments didn't account for what I came into this life with: the experiences, cellular memories, and energetic Remembrances.

It did not allow for what Simone Wright, calls "First Intelligence," in her book of the same name. This is not "a product of the human brain or intellect.... It is an innate and powerful guidance system that ranges from the wisdom inherent in the tiniest strand of DNA to the advanced intelligence discovered in the chambers of the heart. First Intelligence is wired deeply in every cell we possess, and it uses our DNA to connect us to and communicate *with* the same intelligence that guides the planets and gives birth to all the stars in the universe."[2]

There are many different schools of thought and research that have documented the capacity of an individual to tap into "information" that was acquired before the current lifetime. It is not my purpose to explore that here. I am sharing it now because it is the only way that I have been able to understand my own experiences.

Yet for such a long time I carried shadows of feeling that I was not the teacher that I am. Even as a "super-elder," when I had more than enough academic expertise and current life experiences to speak to anyone, I entertained the presence of this shadow.

2 Simone Wright, *First Intelligence*, New World Library, 2014, p.13

From Separation Comes...

What was it that I needed from this experience of loss?

When I look back to see what I am able to acknowledge now, I see a bigger picture.

I needed the understanding of having forgotten the truth and then finding the way back in (the return), following the path, step by step. This is what has made me a great "bridge builder." A bridge builder is someone whose life experience gives them the means to be a wayshower for others. Someone whose being creates a template that others can use in their own journey to remember the truth. Often, we don't recognize ourselves as bridge builders. Certainly not when we are going through those experiences that develop this superpower. It often takes someone else to point out the value of our life path—especially the parts where grit and gristle created scars.

If you are alive, you have scars.

There are many bridges that can be built across countless canyons. Maybe you are a bridge builder. Has there been a life journey you've taken, a path of healing or discovery that is now an energetic framework for others? It isn't necessary that you do this as your work in the world. The very fact that your bridge exists makes it available for someone else to use in their own life. Think of it this way. Your lived experience creates a blueprint that exists as part of the energetic field of which we are all a part. So, where needed, your blueprint is now accessible to assist others. You don't even need to write a book to make it available!

The Act of Forgetting

Guidance stated to me: *The act of forgetting is what we are here to review. You did not have to feel unloved.*

But I did feel unloved. The entire arc of my life went forward from the act of forgetting. I felt desperate to remember. As if that held the secret code to my life.

I was a wise woman at a young age, and nobody could tolerate it. Least of all me. There were things I *knew*. The pull of knowing that I now understand as *intimations of remembering*. But the fog of forgetting was very strong.

I wasn't comfortable in my own skin, and certainly not in my life!

This led me to choose a double major of English and psychology at university. This was one of those parallel moments where the ghost of Remembrance acts as guidance for our choices.

I studied authors who were exploring life—anything that could bring me closer to what I was longing for in myself. Then I continued in graduate studies at Cold Mountain Institute in Vancouver, British Columbia, opening the channels with Humanistic Psychology. Did I know, really, what I longed for? I don't think I did. I certainly would not have called it love. That felt far too simplistic to me. I didn't know anything then about the power of love—only the power of my mind to track and create problems, to try and understand myself from the essence of what I thought life was about.

I could say I got off track, but I don't think so. I believe this was the "soul-track" that I had chosen, so that I could learn about how I was to move forward. One choice took me to the next. I went from therapy to all of the alternative ways of working with people (and myself): Bioenergetics, Hakomi, Gestalt, Jungian Psychology, Transpersonal Psychology. I created workshops that I called The Inner Journey.

I had hints and support that I followed along the way, such as Gene Worth (my vocal teacher), who provided me with an experience of love, support, and connection.

But there was still something hidden and untouched. When I discovered Guided Imagery and Music (the Helen Bonney Method of Guided Imagery and Music, a.k.a. GIM) I felt like I was home. In fifteen months, I completed the two-year training course to be credentialed as a Fellow and was invited to become part of the small national training staff.

On the personal side of my GIM training, I immersed myself in my inner world with images and experiences that gave me more clues to follow. My ears opened to hear other levels of vibration where I could track energy and receive information. The music itself brought me beauty that I had ignored for lack of understanding of what it could hold. Beauty was key, because it took me to a deeper appreciation of something I could not measure or truly name. It had a physical resonance, and I found it expanded my awareness. From GIM, I discovered Reiki, and with Reiki, there was an inner quieting and more discovery. The dimensions hidden from the outer world began to make themselves known to me.

No Space for Remembering

Psychology was my chosen field of study and then my first work in the world. I say it was a choice, but there was really no feeling of choosing one thing over another. It simply had the most potential for reconnection with parts of myself that felt lost to me. And it did, in its way. But what was missing in that world was love. Psychology could not bring me *back* to that feeling of connection because that connection had always been a fundamental part of who I am. It never had left me. *I had left* it in forgetting.

Psychology didn't have a place for remembering.

I suppose the spiritual path is a way to find it, but this often doesn't work very well, either. For many people, the spiritual takes them out of themselves, with a belief that God is *out* there and that if they obey all of the rules they will be loved. If they meditate or pray long enough and in the right way, they'll be blessed.

I already knew how to follow the rules. This isn't the essence of life.

Rules and regulations and shoulds and ought tos. I didn't need more of that.

It didn't give me the love I craved.

Yet the path of your personal journey through life is to claim what you had willingly (even if unknowingly) turned away from. And how, if you are a radical explorer and ready to open to the greater mysteries of life, you can receive this Remembrance of your connection for all time.

This was Beverly's experience in one of the meditation sessions I held. She came to it feeling mired in self-doubt and concern. As she sat in the energy of what was spoken and shared and then in the silent space of meditation, she was able to drop her concern and settle into herself. She felt love and she felt loved. Her face glowed afterwards when she shared what she was experiencing.

Is that spiritual, or is it something different? Confusion enters as soon as you call out something as being spiritual, because, in fact, you create separation. *This* is spiritual, and *that* isn't.

How do you determine that? Who is the arbiter?

Which brings me to people's longing to experience bliss, believing that to be the height of spirituality.

What are people looking for when they say they want to feel "bliss"?

At the start of their journey, many people want relief from whatever they feel caught in. They imagine that bliss is the place to go to not feel discomfort.

Perhaps it is. It's just not the place to stay if you wish to be engaged in life.

To be in a state of bliss implies a singular state of undifferentiation. It is unbounded, which means that being in a state of bliss isn't actionable. You cannot initiate action from a state of bliss. As you can imagine, this creates all sorts of issues in everyday life. How do you pick up the kids from school, conduct a team meeting, or figure out your budget?

The answer is to bring connectedness into everyday life. If you want to create and manifest with it, the experience of remembering must be alive in you.

The experience beyond separation that allows us to live in the world in our full capacity requires embodiment. The vibration of love is physical; it is felt in the body. It is neither mental nor emotional, although those are a part of it, because we are not separate from those aspects of ourselves.

"The body is in the soul, the soul is not in the body."
Hildegard of Bingen, *Book of Divine Works*, Part 1, Vision 4

And as my friend Nancy Swisher says, "...the dynamic spiritual energy (flows) through us. Do we leave our body to tune into this infinite energy? No, we do not! ...We don't bypass the physical in order to access the spiritual."[3]

My journey continued. I was still a seeker. I had not yet remembered. Yet when the student is ready...

But the timing is not exactly up to us. Dawn had not yet entered my life. So, hold that thought.

3 Nancy Swisher, *Sunday Spirit* newsletter, 2024

Shame Is Not the Truth

At the end of my studies at Cold Mountain Institute, I did an internship at their center on Cortes Island: three months in residence with encounter groups, personal confrontation, bodywork, and daily personal growth sessions of various sorts. The facilitators were luminaries of the Human Potential Movement. They had written countless books, taught all over the world, and were considered masters in their domains.

The theme that ran through it all, especially in the encounter groups, was to find the places that were hidden and shameful. This was what was applauded. It was how you could receive the blessing of the group leaders and therefore the approval and the "love" from the participants. If you didn't find those places, you were confronted as hiding out, unwilling to be vulnerable.

So often, I didn't know what to share. I believed it was because I was out of touch with myself and my emotions. I certainly knew the perspective that we hide parts of us that feel shameful, and the need to bring them into the light.

I'm not sure how often I came up with something because of the expectation that there must be issues to address, and how often whatever I brought up was real and true *for me*.

The love (read that as approval) came at great cost. It was only our wounds that were celebrated. There was no dignity of the soul.

The radiance of each person's inner being—what was greater than their personal issues—was nowhere in the picture.

Remember, these were famous teachers and therapists. I was "seduced" by the confluence of their expertise and my lack of trust in myself.

My capacity for discerning what I needed came much, much later. Vulnerability through confrontation didn't serve me. It was forced by expectation and the unwritten group rules. What I needed was something else entirely. My journey was about surrender, but not to the group, or to others' expectations. It was surrender to myself and the greater life force that pulsed through me. This is a kind of vulnerability where you don't know what's next, when you have stepped away (willingly or not) from all that is known and familiar.

The Two Paths

There are two paths of surrender one can take on this journey. The first path is usually done without awareness, as you defer to the powerful, charismatic leader who wants you to "reveal" yourself. Their intentions may be "good." It's simply that they come from an old paradigm—one that sits in a worldview of separation.

The other path offers an experience of connection and potency, being *of* the Universe, not just in it. Your surrender is to inner truth, that is, to God within you, because this is where you experience being *all that is.* Fundamentally, your individual consciousness is enfolded in the unified field of consciousness—the Universe. In other words, as in a hologram, your particular piece of the puzzle contains all the pieces of all of the puzzles.

In the act of being born, you don't lose wholeness. You "forget" it! Later, when you make an energetic quantum leap, activating the blueprint that has remained intact in your cells, you remember this original truth. It happens in a moment. It is not linear (which is why I call it a quantum leap). In fact, it is a complete paradigm shift, where old beliefs dissolve and fade away.

I took the first path. So I know it, through and through. When you feel this first kind of vulnerability, you give up something about yourself. Even though it feels like you are coming home, because what was hidden is given air, there is something that is also given up. There is a trade-off. It's what I did in my graduate program. I learned the language of encounter groups and of how to "process" myself.

The true path is not to stay hidden—of course. The big picture is to stand in your power and your glory, where your ego doesn't run the show, *and* you are a partner in co-creating with the Universe. And since, after all, this was my journey, there was something for me to learn in taking this route.

I needed space to experience my fear of being seen. I uncovered and healed patterns of grief and mistrust of the world. I learned to share my deep hidden places with others. I allowed myself to show up and be seen.

And there was, of course, still more to discover.

11

The Teacher Appears

That first class I attended with Jane and Sid, held in that private home, is embedded in my memory. Dawn worked with us through what she called energy transmissions. We would sit in meditation, focusing inside in silence, so that we could receive these transmissions that she communicated through touch and with her eyes. Each sitting was about half an hour. There were four sittings each day.

Richard was her partner at this event. His energy transmissions came through his words. He spoke about the new energy frequencies that were coming onto the planet and how people around the world were feeling an inner "calling" to be part of this. Dawn would focus on Richard, holding a high frequency of energy. This allowed Richard to speak with a clear focus, from his connection with Source.

Dawn went around the room and, as before, looked into our eyes, touching each of us in the center of our chest.

Afterwards, as we each shared what had happened, the majority of the participants reported profound experiences of inner Remembrance. Not so the *homeowners*. They kept to themselves—they were difficult to read.

Something kept feeling off in the group. The feeling of separation was palpable; the homeowners' faces were creased with anger. The expansion that the rest of us felt was being limited. If I think of it in terms of frequency, the attitude of the hosts was dissonant to what was being created. Instead of flow, there was disturbance.

Dawn asked Richard to write about what was happening and what was needed, so that he could allow his inner voice to flow through the written word. Then Dawn stopped him and said that she felt she was hiding behind his words. Instead, she needed to bring through what was true in this situation.

She spoke. It was with so much love.

As someone who had both participated in and led dozens and dozens of workshops and seminars, this was beyond anything that I could have imagined. There was no judgment. Only the truth of the differing frequencies. And that the group could not move forward in the way that was possible for us.

Dawn was ready to take us all to a different place to meet, and Jane offered the use of her home. But instead, the homeowners left. The rest of us were able to come together in a way of connection that astonished us all.

So, the hosts left their own home. They left the seminar because their energy was not in sync with what Dawn had brought forth within the rest of us.

That is not to say that everyone else was easily able to stay with the frequency. For example, there was the woman who wanted Richard as her lover.

She thought that it was she and not Dawn who should be in partnership with Richard. It was what she "got." Those were the days when people spoke about channeling, about what they had received from guidance, or spirit, or their guides or angels. Oh my, there was so little discernment about what was true or not! Egos got involved and everyone was quick to spout off what they had "heard."

Some people's egos ran wild, imitating Dawn in her way of listening and speaking. But Dawn had been doing this for years, and she had come to a place of such refinement with it. She was grounded in a way that I rarely saw so-called spiritual people inhabiting. She was funny and fun. What came from her words impacted my body in a way that I came to discover was the feeling of truth. I didn't know it then. I only knew that

I felt wonderful. Not high, not untethered. Yet with a feeling of love and fullness and ease in my body, and a felt sense of being connected inside myself.

It was the first time that I could remember feeling that solid. I was used to feeling some kind of emptiness inside—space that was just there. It didn't leave me; we coexisted. I was so used to it that the absence of feeling empty was startling. I noticed it immediately.

What had been empty was no longer so. This was something indeed.

I had never met anyone who was so trustworthy. That she was willing to upend her entire seminar in the service of truth gave me a profound respect for her. Here was someone I needed to be with.

What Is Love?

Love...

Is the Reconnection with Presence—your own truth.

Is Communion, the realization of this union.

Provides Gestation to allow for building this relationship.

Is founded in Gratitude, in the fullness of what is available to you in each moment.

Thrives in Circulation: giving/receiving; the inhalation and exhalation of the breath; Thanks...Giving.

Is an ode to Joy.

Vibrates as the fuel for all creation.

Is Energy.

Flows without cessation.

Resonates as the energy of truth.

Is the Expression of your essence.

Moves you forward: Unlocks, unblocks, unsticks.

Reveals the blueprint for your life.

Brings insight into what really matters to you.

Contains and nourishes the vast field of unlimited potential.

Sustains you.

Creates.

Is you.

Is me.

Remember who you are.

LOVE.

Beyond romantic love, underlying the love between parent and child, between spouses, siblings, friends, and neighbors, there is the energetic vibration of love. This essence of Unconditional Love lives in every cell of your body, dormant, available, and ready for activation. Awakened, it is the fundamental element of creation.

Unless you feel love and believe it in your own body, you cannot change how you live and what you do. When self-doubt is generated, it creates a constant state of tension because you doubt these intimations of love. At its core, self-doubt is the denial of love that is actively available to you.

I'm talking about Self-love, the kind that doesn't have anything to do with another person. Love that is cell-penetrating, grander, more magnificent than any human could contain or provide.

If your heart is closed down in fear or self-doubt, you aren't able to receive that Love. You stay with negative patterns, your limiting beliefs or old wounds. *That focus keeps alive the negative experiences of your life.*

However, when you are able to experience Love as a physical, tangible feeling in your body, as a vibration in your very core, an incredible strength takes hold within you.

This is the invitation the Universe is always extending to you. Receive it. Breathe it in.

People don't realize where they turn away from love. They don't see how their thoughts coalesce around being unloved or unlovable. They search for healing, believing that it has to go on and on. They roll through modalities and practitioners, looking for magic. They look for the partner who will provide this, even making someone fit into the picture of who they think this is.

What if, instead, you opened to love within yourself, by remembering your original connection?

In this connection is the experience of Unconditional Love.

Love changes everything in an instant. The frequency

of Unconditional Love is available to us all. It has a cellular impact, allowing the cells to vibrate at a higher frequency than what exists in the frantic search for power, prestige, and yes, even healing. It is the quiet voice within you that whispers what is true.

I urge you to listen to it. Can you get quiet enough inside so that you can hear? What do you notice? Is this difficult? Are you holding fast to what you have been taught to believe and, at the same time, fear to be true?

When you allow yourself to rest in silence, mind chatter settles. Another truth emerges—one that cannot be accessed through linear thought. Linear thought keeps us on the known tracks. Anything else gets relegated to woo-woo, or what is not logically rigorous.

Beyond the waves of emotion that we conflate with love is a feeling of radiant well-being. It is experienced in the body. It arises from the experience of being connected with our own heart. It is out of this that *true creativity* emerges and becomes accessible.

True creativity is made possible by going off-track, off the well-worn paths of what you already know. It demands stepping away from what is familiar. It demands a recognition of the qualitative difference between something you know because you have been taught, and what you remember as your brain connects with your heart in this new way of being.

It feels different in your body.

Love is available through so many avenues. You may remember it when you allow yourself to feel something that you have both longed for and pushed away, perhaps for your whole life. There have been so many times when I've been in a therapy or mentoring session with a client, and I could *see*, I could *feel* where this Remembrance lived inside—where that preciousness had been pushed into hiding. I could feel the truth of it, so why wouldn't they? Why wouldn't they allow themselves to feel it? To believe? I could feel the truth of it, but they could neither feel it, nor believe it.

But of course, I could not make them see what I saw.

And yes, I also remember how many times I chose to only see what was wrong with me and my life—and buried myself there.

What Else Is Possible?

The truth is that it isn't a matter of being broken and fixed. *This was the journey I was to take.* How could it have been otherwise? Who would I be if all of that had been different?

This is a crucial realization. It's so important that I ask you to pause for a moment and really consider it for yourself.

You cannot circumvent it or avoid it. Without going on your own journey, however that has looked, you would not otherwise be able to learn whatever it was you were here to learn for your own development.

You must make the journey! Then, you get to become the witness to it, to see it from the space of time that is beyond time. That may feel impossible at this moment. I understand. If it feels too far from your current experience, that's okay. Perhaps leave it in the background for now—as something to return to in your awareness when you are ready.

This is what is asked of you if you are to claim your life. To realize that healing is not all that is needed. *It's not enough.* More importantly, your focus on it derails remembering by keeping the spotlight on you needing to be fixed.

There is a distinction between healing and fixing. Healing has a quality of gentleness. It happens from the inside, out. Often, it arises out of new learning or discovery. In contrast, you fix something that is broken or has something wrong with it. Most of the time, though, they are thought to be interchangeable.

The beliefs around healing are deeply entrenched. *It's never-ending. You are never finished. There's always more. It takes a long time.*

Laurie Seymour

What if this isn't the truth?
Something else is possible.
Love is possible.

14

The Initiation

Five of us, along with Dawn and Richard, traveled down Highway 285 from Denver to The Baca Grande. Leon, Dennis, Ian, Jane, and I were chosen to be part of this experience. Seven souls together. As soon as we arrived, after a five-hour drive, stopping along the way to buy groceries in Conifer, we had to drop everything and gather in the living room of Townhouse 18, one of the original homes built in the heart of The Baca Grande. There was no unpacking or settling in or even dressing for the occasion! The non-perishable groceries were left on the counter.

The Baca Grande is a land grant adjacent to the town of Conifer in the high desert of southern Colorado, known for its diverse spiritual communities scattered over many hundreds of acres. Months prior to this, Dawn had been invited to visit and had bought a townhouse. This was where we gathered.

So much had led to this moment, from receiving the invitation from Dawn to be initiated, to addressing the utter disbelief that I could ever manifest what was needed to step into the invitation. There was no way that I would miss this invitation, so it became a grand opportunity to trust. I had been waiting my entire life for this. I was invited, and that meant that there was a way for this to happen.

And it did—magically, miraculously, yet also through practical actions that I took in the physical world. I was moved to work with my relationship with Sid to bring us into a deeper truth of our purpose together. He was not part of this particular moment. This was my time.

The Energies were present and insistent for what was to come. Dawn always referred to her experience of connecting with Source and receiving frequencies, as "the Energies." She spent years of inner world training as a Master in becoming intimately familiar with her embodied experience of this.

In this case, these were the Energies of initiation, brought into her physical body so that she could make a quantum leap available for each of us who were gathered.

Let me shift gears to explain a bit.

Everything is energy. The cells of the body are both receivers and transmitters. As the cells receive higher frequencies of energy, which are essentially encoded activators, higher levels of consciousness are made accessible, and health (on every level) improves. The evolutionary process unfolds in its next step.

Frequencies of energy are brought together for a particular purpose. Dawn's gift was initiation. She had long been able to access ever-higher dimensions of consciousness in her body and, through her own physical vehicle, make them available to others.

During the entire drive, Dawn had been receiving energy, and she could no longer put herself on hold. We sat and began. I don't remember who was initiated first. I only remember my own experience.

Dawn asked me to look into her eyes, to maintain eye contact and, as best as possible, not to blink. I felt waves of energy pouring from her eyes into me, creating sensations not only in my eyes, but through my entire body. This energy was filling my body with a presence that was undefinable, and yet utterly *real*. I felt myself—my Self—receive this energy. I felt the tangibility of my existence.

As I looked into her eyes, she asked me what I saw. I hesitated. I saw her face transform into mine: I was looking directly at her, but only saw *my* face; her face had changed shape and form, becoming mine. As I told her what I saw, she then told me that she was seeing her face when she looked at me. She told me that this was the nature of our relationship and of how we were to work.

The initiation was to mirror my way of being with her in the years to come. It was also the means of finding the truth of myself.

This was the beginning of my new life, one where the authority that doubt had in my system began to vanish—doubt about my right to be alive, doubt as to whether or not I was someone worthy of loving, doubt as to who I was and why I was here.

All that doubt because I had not known that I could remain connected with my father and feel his love, alive within me.

This was the moment. It was when the forgetting and the remembering came together. Where turning my back and returning home became one. It was as if there had been no time in between, and yet a lifetime had taken place.

With Dawn I was able to finally, finally, finally feel myself. Myself. And my Self. The connection was brought together again. This is the way in which what had seemed broken was made whole.

The Gift of Doubt

Doubt and knowing. I recommend the knowing side highly! Yet my journey with doubt was what enabled me to recognize and to feel where others get stuck. Or where they trip and fall down. Then comes the beauty of standing upright, the light alive in their eyes, the knowing of the truth. That was how this teaching was unfolding.

The practice of connecting with my inner guidance in order to work with doubt blossomed. There are many places in this book where I ask myself questions or invite you to ask questions of yourself. This process of inner inquiry is what I call Inner Research. I learned about using questions while being in the correct frequency. I use this as a focal point to bring through guidance from that part of myself that is the Universal Field, of Source. The Universal Field is the infinite expanse of energy and potential that connects all of creation, serving as the Source from which guidance and wisdom flow.

I sit, take a breath, ask about how I am to work with doubt, and begin to write.

 These are the moments when you are once again replicating that childhood pattern of looking outside for your validation—really, for your love. Realize that others cannot do this for you because they are engaged in their own situations. There is nothing that they can offer to you in the way of validation. There is nothing to be concerned about with this. There is only the need for acceptance of what is. At these times, you must turn inwards,

to what connects you with the vibration of Unconditional Love. This is what will carry you back to yourself. It is what is necessary so that you can do the work that is yours to do. Each person has a different expression and a different purpose to fulfill. Do not concern yourself with how or whether the others do this. You cannot know the purpose that they carry as long as you are disconnected from your own. Your purpose is to reveal the truth. The truth is simple to behold—the experience and understanding which everyone longs for, seeks, goes after, and tries to grab hold of—all of them truly want only one thing: Love. When that love is balanced and received, when they know that what they need is so available, then life expands. What if there had never been a person in their lives who loved them? Then you become that person, holding fast to the vision of their true heart. You carry that in your hands, recognizing the value of the true heart before you. They are one-of-a-kind, like no other before them or after—the special nature of the way that God enlivens this one.

 You speak of the breath of God. God breathes life into each being. So it is that the breath is everlasting; it is continually replenished. Each breath that we take, every day and throughout our physical time on earth, is a reconnection with that original breath. The longing, the forgetting, the mistrust, and the doubt: these are all a manufactured unreality that vanishes in a moment. Do not be afraid of what is to come. For this is indeed what you are here to write of: the story that each person longs to be true yet hesitates to believe. This is the power and the glory. It is the truth that is to be shouted from the rooftops, and also needs to be heard, whispered to those who would hear. You are to find those who are ready to hear and to initiate them.

Here is a question for you, my reader. Where does what you have just read take *you*? Notice how your body feels. That's a good place to start.

You always have been and always will be loved. Truly, effortlessly, without trial and effort. In fact, if efforting is part of your "show" (as it was long a part of mine), know that it only exists so that you can become aware of what is NOT needed.

Turn the page, take a breath. Receive that breath and all that it has to offer to you. Would God have made it difficult for you? Are you supposed to suffer?

We can get so attached to suffering.

So, what is suffering about? Why illness? Why disease? Why injustice? Why the common variety of meanness that we experience so often these days?

We suffer as we forget, and, in the forgetting, we pull away from our connection. From the knowing that we are fundamentally each a part of one another, and of *all that is*. I know there are places where this message will not be received, but these are not the people who can hear. This is what I know:

You have nothing to convince anyone about and nothing to show anyone. You are. Simply that. And with this simple message you carry your purpose.

Why Me?

This is the question that was alive in me so often. *Why me?* What is special or unique about me that I am here in this moment with this task that I have been given?

Here is what I was given in my inner dialogue with these questions.

You are being given this task of writing this book because you are the one who is to reveal this. You have come to this place in your life where the revelations are like the stars by which you navigate your journey. There are those who are ready to receive this message, and for them, you must write it. For you, too, for you are one of them and this will give you freedom to know the truth. It is indeed the way that the truth of your own life will be revealed to you. *This is the story of the one and the many.*

So, what it is that you receive, others will also, in turn. What others claim to learn, so too will it be your learning. All of life can be viewed through the lens you have been given. There is more, much more, that will be made clear to you. And by which your freedom will be realized. There is nothing more important than this. To this you must dedicate yourself above all else.

What is it?

It is your realization of the truth of this message and the path upon which it takes you. This is the path you have walked since before this time began and it is one that is ready for fruition. Just as you have become comfortable in following the vibration as you speak (for that has indeed taken place), now it is time for you to feel the movement, the flow of the vibration of your pen as you write the words which come through you. Do not think for a moment of anyone and what they might think of you, of how they may feel about what you share. This is not your responsibility. Your only responsibility is to bring through the truth of the vibration into the written word. What exists as vibration manifests through your pen, your computer, your voice. It is now the time to bring to manifestation the preparation and training which have been given to you through the initiations you have received.

 Everything has come together. There is no behind and there is no holding back. As you step, feel for the ground beneath you. The next step may feel like you are stepping into air. But go ahead; step firmly and the ground will rise to meet you. This is the way that it is, and this time is to show you this new aspect of your expression and the way in which it is manifested. Let yourself receive it, dear heart, for your heart has long desired this to the exclusion of anything else. What was lost has been found.

You can now recognize the importance of this time of forgetting. You have remembered how it is. Never think that this time of forgetting was wasted. It was not. It is what allows you to be with the others who have forgotten—those precious souls who have the same feeling of love lost that you have known. It will be through this process that you help bring them to the light.

The Invitation

There was a feeling of great joy in my body as I wrote this next part. It was as if the page was filled with light, the words transparent to the light. Remember writing with disappearing ink? Well, this is the opposite of that. It was writing with *light*.

 As you write, the light appears through the written word. There is a dance that is apparent. It is an invitation to dance with you. To celebrate that love can be recovered and remembered. Is this not something in which to delight? From which to make magic? Words are but a vehicle through which the energies can flow. You have been deepening your understanding of the power of the symbols in your times of meditation. So too shall you discover more about this part of the process, of how you are to work with the symbols which you have been given, for the symbols have been imprinted upon you through each of your initiations. They are sealed on your skin and live in your cells. Nothing else matters but that you give voice to what is needing to come through.

For this is the next page, so to speak, of the journey of your book, which has come through tonight and must be brought through to completion. The breath of God that began your journey will find its way into your words. And through your words into the hearts of those who have longed for this day. Somewhere within you was the memory. That is why you have been searching. It's the same for the others. All of those who are searching are looking for only one thing: to reconnect with this love. To remember. You have long been writing these words, but now you understand the magnitude of what they mean. The pieces have come together. The halves have been united. All of the doubt, disappointment, concern or worry is like the out-breath that dissipates in the wind. For you have come home. And in the writing, you will be given the means to communicate and to claim all that you have remembered. Isn't it simple? Isn't it simply elegant? This is why you have come to this place and why you must write.

For in the writing, you will be able to see the pieces that were hidden from your view. The light will grow stronger. You will feel more and more ease in your writing for it will be as simple as following each step, flowing from one to the next. That is how effortless it will be. You will see. You have seen. And now you may sleep to be filled with the love that is ever present and ever available. You are loved. You are love. And so is everyone else.

What more is there for me tonight?

 See to it that your body is relaxed tonight so that you can receive the new energies which we are making available to you. We are with you, and you are with us. You have never been alone and now you can rest, assured of this. Let nothing pull you aside from this realization. We have given you a new infrastructure so that it will become easy to sit still within this. Everything will be different from this day forward. You have done what has been asked of you.

This is the time for more, for your next step. You realize that there is always a next step. It is new. This is why what has been done before is the before. There is much that is to be given and much for you to receive. Now begin. Today is a new day. In this new day, the recognition of what has gone before can be celebrated. There is no space for mourning what did not happen with anyone in your life. The essence of what you received is what is to be celebrated. Look at it this way: your ability to know the truth is rooted in your experience of those moments of love. There is nothing else that is to be contemplated. These are the seeds that have sprouted. Now the watering begins in earnest so that the roots may spread. The roots are the foundation. Your words are the flowers, the berries, the fruit of the vine. They nourish in beauty and in substance. Think of manna from heaven, and of the wedding at Cana, of abundance ever flowing. These are the images, the themes that will run through your book. Let us begin.

Where Was the Truth?

Haven't we all known a time when love seemed to vanish? Maybe not in childhood. Perhaps you felt it when your best friend moved away, when your spouse left, or when a loving marriage fell to the wayside from neglect or being taken for granted. So it is with life. Time rolls onward, things change, and we, if we are focused on wanting to find love *in our outer world*, neglect to attend to where it was rooted in the first place!

Religion was supposed to offer the demonstration and experience of love as a reminder of where we came from. Instead, it bound itself to a stance of maintaining its own authority to determine right and wrong. It insisted on its moral authority, conflating the Divine with what was human.

Truth wasn't part of the picture.

Where there was love, love thrived. Remembrance was sustained. There was no forgetting. Where there were rules, where life was marshalled into right and wrong, opinion and control, there was no place for love to exist. Forgetting became the norm. This became our way of life—pockets of truth amidst masses of doubt. Where the crossover existed, where love had existed in the physical world, so there lived a memory that birthed the urge to search, the push to discover. When love existed and stayed constant, the human self learned to nourish itself. It didn't doubt its ability to love or to be loved.

And it still could exercise its ability to choose.

We need experience in the outer world. It is why we come into being. To explore, to learn, to feel what is possible, to evolve and grow: all done in service to a greater expression of the consciousness that fills humanity.

Where love existed and then vanished, as it did in my life, great doubt filled the vacuum. I remember the love that was given, and when it no longer existed in the world around me, I could only search outside for it. I had no understanding of how to look for it inside because my memory of this original state of being had shut down.

Another possibility is present when there never was someone to anchor love—someone to embody the energy and remind you of what you had received when you came into this life—and that is the breath of God.

Of course, God still exists. God is in everyone. But without the experience of a physical anchor of connection, we interact with our intimate others without the experience of love. The Remembrance of our original connection fades, and we focus solely on experiences of our physical world: patterns of striving for outer success, of loneliness, addiction, following outer authorities, and more.

Awakening begins with a glimmer of awareness that there is more. More to life and more that is possible to experience. It's the beginning of the Hero's Journey, the metaphoric Search for Self.

 In your father's passing, you felt lost, the odd duck, left out by virtue of being different. So it is that you continued. Your path became one of a struggle to remember. But because you had been left, you left the Remembrance, you forgot. What remained was the feeling of having had something that you no longer had. Then, because you no longer had it, you began to doubt that it ever existed. This was the trajectory of your life: love—loss—forgetting—doubt—search.

Original doubt, like original sin, makes us fear for our worthiness and our ability to be loved.

The loss of my father and his Unconditional Love had a great impact. The larger story, though, is about forgetting my *original connection with Source.*

Well, seek and ye shall find. I spent years in the search. Who becomes a psychotherapist unless you feel that there is something to fix? I desperately craved what I believed to be validation. The more I sought validation—approval, really— the more it eluded me.

You cannot find validation when you feel empty.

Memory is such a funny thing. It is a trickster, piling pieces on top of others. Layering bits of itself into other memories: disconnected pieces that are later put together to try and represent a whole. So that when you think that you are remembering something, you've only moved into a new illusion—one that threatens to take you someplace other than where you intended to go. It is important to understand that memory will always be partial. It will never be enough, nor will it ever capture the whole. We cannot rely on it to bring us to the truth. It cannot do that, simply because of its very nature.

Something as critical as the original moment—the grace of our connection—must be claimed.

Our Original Connection: Held Within Love

Our original connection comes in the breath of God. It is the original moment when your soul enlivens the physical body so that you can relish the experience of physical life. There is no separation from yourself. Love simply IS.

This is our original blessing. I love the feeling of it and the light it brings. It lets us know that we need no intercessor; no one to be the interpreter of this experience for us. Whole religions sprang up from the notion that someone stood between us and God. They were not there to remind us of our connection. Or rather, they were there as long as the reminder didn't interfere with their position of control.

Your journey in life is the conscious remembering of this original connection. Everything comes from here and proceeds from here. It lives moment to moment. When you remember, all is well. Life flows. You feel aligned and *in love*. That is, *held within love.*

Remembrance is active and engaged. It is not static. In the Old Testament, the Hebrew word for remember is *zakar*. It speaks of the necessity of actively engaging with whatever is being remembered. To *zakar* is to use all of you in the process: your whole body and self. Contrast this with memory, which is a passive, largely cognitive process. You *receive* Remembrance, which is both an active state and an attitude that welcomes something new.

Yet something gets in the way. You get complacent or distracted. You become comfortable and, in that comfort, lose consciousness. You begin to act by rote instead of with awareness. Patterns settle in.

As soon as you step away from being conscious, you begin to suffer, because instead of acting aligned with your heart, ego jumps to take control and must state its case. Ego, which had been happily coexisting with the Presence within, now thinks it has to beat its breast and announce itself as master of the Universe. You stop listening to Presence. You no longer act in accordance with your highest good. You become passive, or the opposite: you charge ahead without clear intention and, most importantly, without inner direction.

You know the familiar dream of falling helplessly through the night? With arms flailing, you try to catch hold of something, anything, that will stop your free fall. You grab hold of whatever looks like it might work. Maybe that will become your next lover or the job that promised you power and glory. Your inner guidance system isn't consulted, mostly because you have forgotten it exists.

Joy? Does that count? Not so much to the ego. The ego just wants to be comfortable. It goes for the lowest vibrational situation that will stop the free fall. It doesn't matter that the frequency is off. It either doesn't notice, or if it does, it explains it away, setting you in motion to override your inner knowing.

Everything changes if, instead, you clear yourself of the tendency to go into unconsciousness. You make the choice to pay attention. You notice when the flow stops. You see yourself in action, whether that be aligned action or active resistance.

Note
There are places where I have included experiments, exercises, or reflection questions for you to deepen your exploration. This is one of them. I invite you to pause to take some time with them. Or return whenever it feels right.

An Experiment

What if you were to take a conscious breath every five minutes? That means, every five minutes you breathe in, knowing, feeling, and receiving it as the breath of God. Do it for thirty minutes a day for a week. At the end of each day, spend a few moments noting your experience. It is especially helpful if you write it down. At the end of the week, decide if you want to continue.

This breath keeps you connected with everything that is.

The situations of your life serve to remind you. But the inference—that is, what you believe to be true, what you infer from your experiences in life—is usually skewed. What you infer usually supports the stories that you've told yourself, which, in turn, are the stories you've been told all along. Stories about how you can and cannot be. About who you are, and who you are not. About what you can do in life and how you are supposed to act. You make your decisions in life based on these inferences!

You either fight against these expectations or you line up in agreement. The fighters are dubbed troublemakers. They stand out in their refusal to go along, but they often band together to form their own system of approval. That's another story, but one you can likely spot in action in the political landscape.

What did I do? I hid out. I didn't go along, but I didn't rebel. I pretended to stay within the rules, but didn't follow them. I didn't stand up in my own defense because I didn't feel strong enough. My mother, on the other hand, always seemed so strong—strong in her desperate holding tight to make things work.

I didn't confront her. I deflected and went around her in my search to experience life. I gave my Italian boyfriend a Jewish last name because I was only allowed to date Jewish boys. I told her I was down the shore with my girlfriend, instead of at the weekend rock concert (Woodstock!).

What happens when you go around an obstacle in order to do what you want? How does it reveal or obscure the path to reconnection?

I still looked outside myself to find the way I was to move forward. Friends became more important than my family, and that took me out of my family structure—so much so that I had neither the support nor the immunity from my own family.

But later, much later, I came into a new family. It was one where we could relate and communicate from an essence that had not before been in evidence—a family born of the Remembrance of our inner connection.

I continue to come to deeper realizations of this connection. Recently I looked at some of those with whom I have walked this path in this lifetime. As I observed each of the precious faces before me, I felt awed by the unique majesty that each of them carries. We are each so different from one another. But we have been willing to surrender to a bigger picture of humanity's relationship with the Universe and the Ascended Masters. (The Ascended Masters are those beings who, having lived physical human lives, are no longer embodied, and are spiritually enlightened. They assist in the evolution of humanity.) And in this, we are united and as one. As I remembered this, I looked at each person with such deep reverence and joy.

When we find those in whose presence we can remember who we really are, we have found our true family.

And yes, sometimes forgetting takes over, even here.

In the moments I have not remembered, I do not feel my place in the world. This is where confusion, doubt, and separation survive. It's like an infection that doesn't completely clear. You can act carefree and confident, and be despairing inside.

This is where the act of comparison is allowed entry. The other day, one of the participants in my meditation sessions shared that she resents "having to meditate; that others can be happy without having to do that." Of course, she can't know the inside of another's experience. I asked her why she continued if she was indeed that unhappy in her meditation. What dictate had she absorbed? This exploration allowed her to feel some space around her tendency to compare herself, and to appreciate all that was hers to experience.

There is great support in being with others who want to remember, who have this as their foundational way of living. It is much more than a spiritual practice. It is a moment-to-moment way of life. Dawn always said that her work could not to be taught as another "technique" for people to add to their tool kit. Truly, it is a way of living. It is a choice that we make to embrace the light instead of hanging back in the dark. Where there is darkness, the light can be brought to bear. Even when there is fear, there is something stronger with which to connect. This is a different way of living. Struggle falls away because there is nothing of truth in it to hold onto. We return to the original blessing. We recognize and remember it.

20

Original Sin Is Really Original Separation

Sidestepping any dialogue about what St. Augustine of Hippo, renowned theologian in the first century CE, termed "original sin," consider that it is our willingness to experience life in all of its forms that creates the dichotomy/duality of forgetting and remembering. Instead of original sin, I prefer "original separation." It feels more accurate and has no judgment.

So, from the original connection (the blessing of the breath of God as the enlivening force of life) comes separation (the movement into life with all of its experiences, its tests, its sorrows, and its joys). I call this forgetting instead of sin. This gives me such a feeling of expansion and possibility instead of the restriction and judgment that is inherent with sin!

Although forgetting indeed is the cause and creation of our suffering, and for this we pay mightily, it also provides a contrasting experience to remembering. In this very distinction, there is a gift. Separation, with its opposing aspect, connection, can give us the impetus to discover how to move between the two. The contrast itself gives rise to remembering, which then becomes an engine of our creativity.

We are incredibly adaptable, resourceful, and creative. We have only to recognize the gift of each, so that we can reconcile what was division, into oneness.

Creativity is not something nice to have, or something that only some of us have. *Our creative expression is the means for reconciliation.* When you shift your attention from excavating the past towards creating with your own life force, a profound shift takes place. You can see what is opening and coming towards you. Your vision brings to you what you long to receive.

21

Creating Your Life

*"All the arts we practice are apprenticeship.
The big art is our life."*

-M.C. Richards, *Centering, in Pottery,
Poetry and the Person*

Do you doubt that life is a creative process that has been designed to work?

Think about it. Your breath has intelligence that knows how to keep you alive without your control or guidance. You don't direct the flow of your blood, nor do you direct the oxygen that nourishes your cells.

You don't have to do that because of this innate intelligence within you.

There are, however, all sorts of ways that you can interrupt the flow of life.

Growing up, I didn't know that life was supposed to work. My parents and teachers never taught me anything about it. They didn't seem to have any idea that life *could* work. Because my family only had Social Security, I learned very early from my mother that life was all about struggle. Even my psychotherapy training was focused on what didn't work: not on what was possible.

Somewhere in me, I knew there was so much more to life and that became the impetus for my own inner journey. When all of the "answers" I encountered outside of me didn't build lasting change, I went inside.

I had never learned to reflect on what was working for me, to acknowledge what I received, and to celebrate change.

Then I discovered how to become quiet, so that I could feel myself. I became skilled in the art of Inner Research, the personal exploration of how life can work. It required discipline to learn how to work with my thoughts so that my inner relationship could grow and become sustaining.

It took me from self-doubt and self-judgment to the freedom of self-discovery and creative manifestation. Instead of needing to be right or worrying about whether I was wrong, I learned that my only source of true direction came from inside.

When your life is aligned from the inside-out, you are continually creating. Nothing is done by rote—not your choices nor your actions. You choose your thoughts and where to place your attention with awareness.

You are the artist. Your life is your creation. Creativity fuels your life force. Your beliefs, thoughts, and actions become the elements for your artistic expression.

If you find yourself caught in an old pattern, see what there is to be learned from it. It may be something in your life designed to show you how you have changed!

Become curious about your life. Don't be afraid to reflect on any part of it. Reflection helps shape your next steps.

Open to what could be possible, even if you are convinced that it's impossible.

Remember, whatever you place your attention on begins to move into form. See your life as your creation, as your work of art.

Shake up your certainty: that action alone creates space for new possibilities. It builds an energetic resonance that draws forth something that is still resting in the unknown and hasn't yet manifested.

Your life is your art. Art is ever-changing. The more you approach life as art, the more opportunity there is for growth and expansion.

This is your remarkable life.

Reflection

How do you feel your life working?

Is life unfolding the way you want?

Are you limiting your options for realizing your dreams?

Do you give free voice to what inspires you?

22

Remember the Truth of Who You Are

The passing of Dawn.

"Leavings" have obviously had such an impact on my life—and this one even more so than others. I had not been in touch with Dawn verbally since she went into silence two months earlier. Those of us who were closest to her had received a few joint communications faxed to us. There was one for the entire group and one for those of us in Denver. During this time, I could not, would not, imagine that this time was other than the next step in her process. And of course, it was. But death was not a part of *my* picture of her process. I could only see her as being intricately part of *my* next steps, of *my* journey.

On June 20, 2008, Dawn made her transition. She was complete with what she had come to do. Her physical life experience was finished. Her body, the vehicle through which she brought the Energies to initiate us into ever more refined dimensions, had been transformed. Her cells were in light. Her time on Planet Earth was fulfilled.

I didn't know how to be with this. I couldn't find my way for a long time. It was more than my grief around her passing. There were also the echoes of my first initiation in The Baca Grande with Dawn, where we saw our own faces as we looked at each other. There was the profound gift and responsibility of being initiated as one of the two Turaya Grand Masters.

I did what I knew to do. Just keep living. Just keep breathing, keep connecting. Continue to listen and follow.

But it was not only grief: it was self-doubt that resurfaced. I didn't know how and even *if* I was to share her work.

Turaya hadn't been present in the public sphere for some time before Dawn's passing. I still taught occasional Turaya Touch© trainings and Turaya Meditation© classes and often did private Turaya Touch© treatments with clients.

It took me two years to answer the inner call to step out. I was often in contact with several of the other people who had met regularly at The Baca Grande with Dawn to receive new energy systems, and we decided to create The Baca Journey. (Later, it became The Baca Institute.)

This group of Inner Researchers had regular gatherings over the years, many of them in The Baca Grande, where my first initiation with Dawn took place. We were dedicated to Inner Research and to uncovering our own potential. We had a passion for inner discovery that transcended dogma, religion, or mental constructs. We wanted to learn about how energy worked, and we wanted that learning to come from our own experience.

The Baca Journey represented that place within each of us that is connected with a greater truth and a desire to discover more about how to live aligned with that truth in everyday life.

The vision that came through was of an online platform that would interconnect those of us who had been with Dawn. Some of us were Turaya Touch© or Turaya Meditation© teachers. Others were artists, businesspeople, scientists, lawyers, and consultants. Some were transitioning from government work into the private sector. The vision was, for those of us who created products or offered services, to come together under the umbrella of The Baca Journey to connect us all, each nourishing the whole. Bit by bit, this arrangement fell apart. But the form kept evolving. Leon (one of the five from that first initiation at The Baca) came forward and stayed for a long time, writing, creating, and sharing.

I finally left Sprint Telecommunications, where I had been a solutions engineer, to move my own enterprise into a self-supporting endeavor. It was to be not only self-supporting, but one that could grow in abundance. I stepped away from Sprint in early 2014, having spent the previous four years pouring my time, energy, money, and spirit into The Baca Journey while still working full-time. I coordinated with my dear virtual assistant, Diana, from airports and on-site customer meetings. I wrote *Friday Focus* blog posts from the road, after early morning calls with Leon, bringing through that week's focus.

Another change came. Leon had other projects that were drawing his attention. He might have continued his collaboration, but it was time for me to take the leap forward from full-time employee, once again, to full-time creator, teacher, guide.

Dawn is with me every day. Now that I have uncovered what I did about my connection with my father, I feel like I have come to a different place with her. I so often feel her in my quiet time and while teaching. She is present in the symbols, the means of working with the light energy that she was given and shared. And most of all, she is present in the breath of God that inhabits my body, taking me step by step, forward, forever forward. I know she is with me. How else could I know about love?

23

To Act or Not to Act

Life didn't always flow, even after big leaps like what happened in initiation. It's not a valid expectation. What is important is that, when it does not flow, you use this awareness to bring your attention to discover what is needed. Curiosity and release of judgment become useful tools.

First, there must be a time of Inner Research so that you can see where you have left home, so to speak: where you left that fundamental remembering of love.

Why would you leave love? Well, the outer world is strong. The pull to believe whatever the outer world reflects to you can defy disbelief, leaving you with an imagined sense of limitation. It's part of your humanness; you feel bound to pay attention to what surrounds you. It is as if your survival depends upon it.

Does it really, though? Because if you attend to the inner relationship, the guidance is available to help shift what you need to shift: to go forward when needed. This brings you right into new dimensions of yourself.

This is a completely different worldview than what most of us have been taught. For most people, the outer world trumps the inner. The outer world is filled with struggle, fear, concern, doubt, competition, and seeking approval. Everyone has an opinion about what you should or shouldn't do.

Yikes! How do children actually make it to adulthood? Well, growing up is what humans are designed to do, but *how* you do it is another story. Look around you. The world certainly seems to be falling apart. Racial and economic divisions, war, climate catastrophes, and terrorism appear to be thriving.

What would it take for something else to rise and take hold?

What is possible must come from a place of inner recognition of who we really are. The reason that things like meditation and mindfulness training have become mainstream is not just because they help you become less stressed. It is that they offer a glimmer of Remembrance. Companies may purchase the training in order to improve the bottom line or to boost employee morale. But what matters to the people in those classes, whether they realize it at first or not, is that they begin to remember something that has been dormant within them: something that once they have an inkling of, they want to explore.

Like Ralph, a client of mine, who had never given any of this much consideration. He thought the outer world was a fearful place, and that he had to compete in order to prove his value. Never did anyone in his life introduce the possibility of an inner world. In his work with me, he has had experiences where he didn't know what the heck was happening. He had no framework to put them in. This actually worked to his advantage because it eliminated his going down the path of long-time spiritual seekers who often mistake air for substance.

As he became familiar with the existence of his own inner world, a whole universe of possibility became available to him that had not been in his awareness. Through his experiences with Turaya Meditation©, he learned how his body could be an access point to his inner guidance system. He became more sensitive to the nuances of both receiving inner guidance and following it. Now, he no longer looks to his outer environment to determine who he is. He has preferences. He has choice.

With the introduction of choice comes recognition of what takes place in a moment in time.

Each moment, you have the opportunity to find yourself with a new choice point. You can elect to keep going the way that you have, or you can shift course. You can upend your life as you know it (it can feel this way, even if you aren't leaving a career, or something equally world-shifting). You can leave a bad relationship. You can walk away from what doesn't value you. You can make different choices. It is up to you.

You can also wait for life to make those choices for you. You might wait until things get so bad that you feel *forced* to change. Maybe you have an accident, and that is the call to pay attention to what is needed. It's as if you wait for the external to bring to the surface what the internal has been trying to say to you.

If you look at everything that happens in your life from the perspective of being co-created by you, then you don't see yourself as a victim. In other words, you have had a part in creating everything that happens. Then, the seemingly awful things that happen can be your way of waking yourself up to see life with new eyes.

Become Visible in Order to Remember

Do you long to remember something that feels just out of your reach?

Take a look.

What's that in your Amazon cart? An invisibility cloak? Or a visibility cape? I'll wait a moment while you check.

I remember the days when I would have given anything to have Harry Potter's invisibility cloak in my back pocket. My desire was to slip about unnoticed and protected.

These days, too, when I'm feeling energetically raw, or riding the white waters of change, an invisibility cloak feels like just the thing.

But after a while (and that bit gets shorter and shorter), the cloak starts to itch and feels sticky. I'm ready to rip it off like a bandage that's caught on an old, already-healed wound.

But conditioning runs deep. Habits strangle, even ones that once seemed so necessary, and clearly no longer are.

Maybe I need to remain invisible. Or maybe I need to just remain small. Then, I can move about, moving into spaces others cannot, because nobody notices me. There's nobody to stop me. I can do what I want without fear of being judged.

Nobody to stop me—except me.

Oh yes. I see.

Here is what I realized.

There has *never* been anybody to stop me. It's always been my own internal pulling back. I got used to disappearing so that I wouldn't face displeasure from my family, my teachers, or my friends. I simply didn't know how to stand up and declare myself.

My balancing act was between feeling safe or feeling good.

I craved being accepted. But mostly, I wasn't. At least not for my inside self, because nobody got to see that.

I felt different. There was just enough of the "big" truth that I remembered that it was hard to believe what I was being taught. I was arrogant in my inner knowing. I'm sure the kids in my neighborhood responded to my inner tug-of-war. Since I had turned my back on myself, how could they not do the same?

Something had to go, so I let go of my inner knowing. I forgot. I swallowed what I was being told even as I fought it. My act of subversion became hiding out because only then did it seem that I was protected.

Appearances, though, are often deceiving. Protection isn't always what you need to feel good.

The cloak of invisibility not only kept me from being seen—it also kept me from myself. A fog of self-doubt crept in, obscuring that seed of inner knowing. I had a choice: nurture that seed into bloom or let invisibility continue to fog the truth.

Here's the amazing gift I discovered. My journey to claim myself was the result of standing outside of the circle.

I didn't feel like I fit in. Believe me, I did try. I'd have walked backwards and upside down if that would have helped.

Yet stronger than craving acceptance was my desire to discover what I felt as *more*. The more that would fade from sight whenever I looked straight at it.

If I had fit in, I would never have gone looking for it. I would have settled.

What is true is that I would never have remembered the truth. Being outside the circle helped me understand that there was more to discover. I had to explore my inner terrain.

Because truth is invisible as long as you are.

This is true for me now: I. DON'T. WANT. TO. BE. INVISIBLE.

It turns out that you have to allow yourself to be seen to discover what has been hidden. You have to be willing to step into the light to find the light.

So, how does a visibility cape work?

A visibility cape gives you superpowers.

Imagine wearing an exquisite garment that inspires the people who see you to be filled with love.

Feel the potency of your words igniting a light in your spouse...your child...your coworker or collaborator.

Picture yourself walking down the street feeling filled with radiance that anyone can see.

Envision your dreams becoming reality, grounded in knowing you are doing what you are meant to do.

Imagine feeling grateful to be you.

That's the power of a visibility cape.

Sheathed in your own true brilliance, your light shines into the dark corners around you. Others hear the invitation to join you because they feel your truth calling to the truth inside of them.

You remember who you truly are, with all your power and glory.

I've set aside my invisibility cloak. (It's in a safe spot in case of need.) These days, because of my own journey, I've stocked my shopping cart full of visibility capes for you. Illuminating words to unlock your remembering. Turaya Meditation© to hasten your remembering. Turaya Touch© to unlock blocked energy and reveal your gifts. Personal guidance and support to bring you home...to yourself.

I offer these because I want to help you to remember the full truth and nothing but the truth. So help me God.

Decide what it is that you really want. Go forward. You only have to take the next step.

25

What Happens When You Take a Fall?

You've just had a fall. An accident. You're shocked, maybe even in need of medical attention.

After you've picked yourself up and attended to yourself as needed, you may start to wonder. What's this all about?

I fell three times in one month. While I don't think any lasting damage was done, I was left bruised and shaken. There was something so innocuous about the way it happened each time—as if I had been simply swept off my feet. Each time, it seemed like a simple bit of clumsiness. When I tuned in, though, I realized there was so much more to discover.

A fall gets my attention. It is a very physical action, shocking my system. I am stopped in my tracks. There is an internal demand that comes with it: I need to pay attention, to look at what I am doing and how I am thinking.

A change in direction and a shift in perspective are needed.

The only way you can determine what is needed is to stop, relax, breathe, and ask yourself questions. Do you remember how, when crossing the street, you learned to stop, look and listen? This is the same.

An accident of any kind can be the doorway to new awareness. Do your own Inner Research to uncover the message. Once the message is understood and integrated, you will feel back in the flow.

Life gives you messages. It is up to you to pay attention to them. Ask yourself questions with an open and curious attitude and let the answers come to you. You will discover your next steps.

Reflection

What is important to know about what has happened?

Look at the areas of your life where flow is not happening. Is there something you need to change?

What are the stumbling blocks in your life right now?

Have you pushed aside an awareness you had, ignoring it in favor of staying the course?

Are you focused on what you need to do?

Is there something you must put into place to support a new alignment?

What do you require in this new time? Is there something new to be put into place?

What do you need to shift in order to reconnect with the flow?

No Blame

It would feel much better (maybe) to blame someone or something, wouldn't it? There's always a likely candidate available! For example, "I was born into the wrong family." "I had a husband who abused me." "I have bad genes and got sick." "My parents didn't support me."

Blame offers you very little, though. As long as you are viewing the world through this lens, there's no way out of the situation (nor into the inner world, for that matter). There is only the continuing drama of blame and suffering.

We see blame so acutely in the political arena today. The focus on opposition brings more of the same, where one side feels the world is a terrible place and only they can fix it. Then the other side looks at the very same world, sees *different* things that are terrible and need to be fixed.

Of course, they are contradictory and opposing. Always, someone wins and others lose. Why? Perhaps because everyone is after the same thing, but hasn't *truly* remembered what that is. So, you stay caught up in what you perceive is wrong.

Your Inheritance

Within the heart of humankind is the breath of God. There is nothing that separates you from this, as in fact, you are this. Then, from the moment you take your first breath, you engage in the world according to your situation and your ability to remember this connection. Maybe you have the experience of love in your physical life as the bridge. Perhaps it wasn't there at all. Or, like me, you lost whoever embodied love for you.

Nonetheless, the breath of God is still alive in every cell of your body. This, then, is the spark that ignites the lifelong search to recover what you lost. To remember what was forgotten.

It really does exist. It's encoded in your cells. It is the primary force from which you come. But you must remember.

How do you remember?

There is a path that you must take in order to claim this inheritance. Ponder the word "inheritance." I used to bemoan the fact that there is no outer-world pot of gold for me to receive when someone dies. I thought about how that would make things easier. What a laugh. That was one of the things that Dawn and I had in common. Neither of us had outer-world support from others. We had to do what was needed on our own. She was so willing to listen and to obey. Life brought her riches, but the Energies had plans for those riches. There were jewels that she had paid for herself. And they were only bought because the Energies stated that they were things that she was to have. There were multiple reasons; each gemstone has an energetic potential and effect. Dawn moved about the world in a kind of "secret service." There were people that she was to connect with who would only be able to "see" her if she came appropriately garbed. This allowed her to be in the circles where she needed to have an impact. She didn't need to have these people as students. Her impact was in the love she brought to them.

My inheritance has come in what I have claimed as my Remembrance of my original connection. This is priceless, beyond any imaginable measure.

28

Recover and Recovery

To recover something, an item, or a state of being, implies something was lost and then was found. To be "in recovery" indicates a process that is undertaken. When someone says that they have recovered themselves, it usually means that they have gotten over something that disturbed their usual state of being. People doing 12-step programs say that they are "in recovery." What is implied is an ongoing process of not only *abstaining* from doing something but actively *embracing* their full potential.

What if we used the word recover as it pertains to love lost? The love that was lost was the original connection. The original connection is the one with the Inner Teacher. It is more than the teacher, though. It is also Mother, Father, God. It is the love from within that carries all of those elements, each a piece of the energetic whole.

I related to God the Father through my physical father. I related to the idea of Teacher through the many teachers that I loved.

This didn't always work out very well. First in high school and then in college, I confused sexual love, especially with powerful men, with the love that I longed for from my father. This showed up in liaisons with more than one teacher.

I did not fully realize the energy of the Mother until I knew Dawn. There were certainly loving women in my life before her. Dawn carried the aspects of both mother and teacher. With her, the teacher aspect was clear and not muddied by sex. It was clean. That was why I was able to come into full Remembrance through the vehicle of that relationship. My willingness to surrender the personal aspects of myself that I had developed over years of thrusting myself into life, controlling, wanting to understand—these were all surrendered in the service of something that I longed for and that I found with Dawn.

Before my experiences with Dawn, I was disappointed, over, and over. The "representatives" that appeared were all lacking in substance and more specifically, in truth. They were not fully conscious beings.

They themselves had not remembered.

So, is this to say that without a Dawn in one's life, there is no chance to reclaim that center of your existence? This cannot possibly be true. There are others like Dawn. It isn't about worshipping Dawn or, in any way, making her the center of focus. It is instead a movement of claiming that which is inherently yours—and that is, no matter the circumstances of your life, to feel loved.

Because knowing that you are loved does change everything. Consider the child growing up in a poor family. If that child grows up feeling nourished in the love of his or her parents, if there is a feeling of security in the village because love exists there in the leadership, then that child has everything that is needed.

From this kind of beginning, choices are available. Decisions about what path to follow are open and unhindered.

In the midst of writing this, I am aware of my back. The middle of my back is hurting so much. What does it need to express? What are the words that come from this pain? I am tight, I am constricted. I am unaligned, or rather misaligned. I want to stretch and expand beyond what I feel the space for.

I ask, what do I need to express?

 You are dear to me. Each sign and signal and pain and breath. All of it, all of you, is dear; you are the one that I have been waiting to receive.

You are the aspect that makes the elements coalesce. This is the aspect of the receiver, who is also the generator and the activator. Nothing in this system of life is passive. It can be relaxed, it can be easeful, but never passive. Passive has no choice, or rather makes no choice. It only takes what comes its way. Look now to see if you have suffered with the act of no action. If you have stayed when your heart has told you to go. If you have feared to step out and then have held yourself back, reined in away from the possibility of danger. Danger only exists in the fear of stepping forward. Danger is aligned with the wondering of what will happen if? What will happen if you don't is a better question.

What will happen if I don't?

 You will have no choice in the result. You will have to absorb rather than express the Energies that have been preparing you for this time.

You are to commit to teaching where you are directed to go and to buy your ticket.

You will indeed be in work mode there. You will be able to feel the fullness of who you are, with nothing to restrict your movement. Hold yourself tall and see if that does not ease the pain in your back.

29

Generator as Initiator

Dawn always said she was the generator of the stars onstage. She was the initiator. That was how she partnered with the Energies as co-creator.

 This is what you do. You picture with your clients the possibilities, not the struggle. When there are struggles that are hampering their remembering, they need to speak of them, to relinquish those struggles for the sake of connecting with a deeper truth about themselves. The gold that you are mining is the truth of the light within them. It cannot be done in words. This is why Turaya Meditation© and Turaya Touch© are so important. It gives them the inner experience of the potential contained in the words. It connects them with the fundamental truth that underlies all else. No longer do you have to quibble with others about whether there is one truth. This is the one truth. This is what each of you seeks to bring into your life. You fear that it is not true. But then something happens that sparks a glimmer, a thought, a memory. This can grow and become strong. Or it can become dormant again, sinking below the level of consciousness that would allow it to become real. These are the choices.

My work is to activate the energetic, felt sense experience of the possibilities. Then the teaching aspect allows people to have a mental understanding of the ways they can interrupt this Remembrance so that they can learn to sustain it. They can undercut it with a thought. They can turn their back on it in judgment. They can deny it right out of existence, at least from their personal realm.

Yet it exists without regard for any denial—or we would not be here. We would have no life.

 Whether or not you acknowledge it, it is what it is. The breath of God continues to keep you alive. It loves and nourishes you. Bit by bit you can discard and deny it. Pain by pain, you can turn your back. This is your choice. It is your right. But it is not necessary. You would still be safe if you were to claim it.

So why not at least entertain this notion? This is your invitation! Your invitation to know that you are loved, you have always been loved, and you always will be loved.

It makes life so much easier. Much simpler.

It's also true that suffering is real. It is not to be diminished or ignored. Instead, it is there so you can see that there is an entire universe in which all of this means something different than you believed. Because your suffering has been your choice, an unknowing one, though it may be.

Not knowing the law (or, in this case, the applicable Inner Law) does not lessen it's impact.

30

How Your Potential Is Governed by Inner Law

Unless you're a lawyer (or someone in need of a lawyer), you probably don't spend much time considering how the law impacts your life. Why would you? On the other hand, learning about *conscious* law connects you with the secrets of unlocking your potential.

There is Outer Law and Inner Law. Each plays a different role in life on this planet. Outer Law addresses commercial, social, and political interactions. Governments create laws to control behavior in the name of establishing order, protecting health and public welfare, and providing safety. Outer Law influences collective behavior and interaction. These laws are written down and codified, so that you know the existing rules to follow as part of society.

Outer Law is governed by other people. It is something imposed upon you as a framework that places limitations and controls on how you live life.

What is the other aspect of this? *Inner Law.* Inner Law is about how life works. I think of it as *conscious law.* Understanding Inner Law opens you to a bigger picture of life that embraces your potential.

Inner Law, which is immutable, affects whether you experience a series of confusing, disordered messes or a grand collaborative dance between the microcosm (you) and the macrocosm (everything else). You may not know it, see it, or understand how it works. Yet your awareness of the way in which Inner Law operates determines your moment-to-moment experience of life. You feel yourself flowing with life when you are following Inner Law.

Inner Law is administered from within you. Adhering to Inner Law strengthens your connection with inner guidance and Creative Intelligence, revealing your next step. *Inner direction is available to you in every moment.* It becomes available when you adhere to Inner Law. You have free will to follow or not. It is your choice.

Following Inner Law is about creating alignment between your inner direction and your outer actions. That takes discipline and fortitude. It takes practice and patience. Alignment requires your willingness to stop, to question, to listen, and to obey.

You begin to master this intimate partnership that is bigger than you alone, where your own creative life force is allied with the Universe's energy of manifestation.

With each step, this alliance becomes more deeply interwoven in your being. You establish a sense of trust in your inner knowing. You know you are on the right track, and your confidence flourishes. You manifest more than you ever dreamed possible.

The gift you receive is a feeling of reverence for life and a deep sense of joy.

Here is the truth: life is designed to work. We just haven't been taught the inner workings! Yet every moment brings you the opportunity to choose how you respond and what action to take. The vastness of possibility—your potential—becomes available when you embrace Inner Law.

So many people claim to know what it is that God has laid down for us to follow. There are churches and holy people striving to sway what you do, perhaps in the name of the "hereafter," but most certainly so that you abide in the present by what they say is the rule.

God's laws, in the realm I am talking about, have to do with Inner Law. That we each have free will to choose our path.

We each have free will to forget and to remember.

This reality changes the game. There is nothing that is imposed upon you. What if you were given the choice to look on your life as one of grace? Then you could see each moment when you had forgotten, when you had turned your back, when you had gone against your own heart. If you see these places as part of your journey, without judging yourself for having them, then you can understand the choices that you made at that moment. Even though at the time, you didn't feel you even had a choice.

Awareness of choice is key. When you begin to experiment with the idea that you were making choices in every moment of your life, you can then become curious about what is happening and what is possible. Curiosity allows you to examine your choices, to look at these times of forgetting and creating struggle for yourself, and to see them for what they are.

You have to be willing to relinquish blame. There is no room for blame when you have activated these curiosity and awareness pathways. You can no longer look at injustice in the same way when you understand the roles that you play in it. Aggressor, abuser, victim, abused, rich man, poor woman.

What could change in the world if you were to remember? How would systems change when the energy holding them in place dissipates?

Personally, we are in need. Globally, we are in need. There is no one who is not impacted; there is no system that is not complicit.

Replenishment from Source

When you forget your connection with Source and give your personal will the lead, you go to your default mode. In fact, you handicap yourself, pushing forward unsupported.

Consider what happens when you hold your breath. Or breathe shallowly, so that you don't bring enough oxygen into your cells. If your breath is the breath and the intelligence of God (the Universe), you deplete yourself of the resources that you need in order to create.

My personal will is strong. I can accomplish many things and have success. But when I operate from my default mode, I cannot access the "inspirational juice" from Source that circulates in me as the energetic fuel of creation.

This is where you hit burnout. Your empire crumbles. Because there is nothing to replenish you when you hit empty.

There is an exchange—a balance of energy—available in each of life's interactions.

Think of the circulation of your breath. The chemical interactions in the blood nourish you, then create another chemical action that feeds the natural world: your exhalation, full of carbon dioxide, nourishes the plant kingdom.

This is the essence of life's exchange.

An Experiment

Pause for a moment right now and take a conscious breath. Picture it moving through your body as light energy. There is no need to direct it. Your breath knows exactly what it needs to do. As you exhale, feel the release of what is no longer needed in your body as the exchange cycle completes. Acknowledge that you are receiving as you give.

As you acknowledge what you receive, you give value to it. There is no need for you to measure what was received. Balance comes in the exchange itself, not in an equal weighting of the elements. *Gratitude for what you receive opens the gate for your own generosity.*

You are an aspect of Co-creative Intelligence. Replenishment comes through your connection with Source. So does co-creation. Co-creation never depletes. Source never imposes itself on you. You always have free will.

The Lessons/The Teaching

The Breath

Life for humans on this planet begins with breath. In the beginning, and before the beginning was God. And God breathed life into humans, so that they would have the means to interact with the outer world, to explore and to demonstrate back to God what life looked like—what it was when it was embodied into differentiation in human form. God made the form so that it would not last, so that it would naturally decay and return from whence it came. This is the nature of everything that God created: the animals, the seasons, all of created matter. The creation that is us was not meant to exist forever as a physical entity. This is important. If we could embrace the natural journey of our physical body as the vehicle that eventually wore out, we would be able to claim the wearing-out part of the journey as the piece of the Divine order that it is.

Unfortunately, most people mistreat their vehicles, not understanding that it is their responsibility to care for them. They do not put in the correct fuel, they let the tank run dry, they do not wash and polish the exterior. They push it beyond its limits. They do not see it as having true value. Then, when the body begins to fall apart, when pain takes over, they get angry and heap abuse upon abuse.

Why would we not want to take care of this transport vehicle that carries us about and allows us to experience so much? And then, for those who long to return to the original oneness, is the path of bodily abuse the way to go back? I have seen it result in going further away from the truth that is their true connection.

Allow yourself to imagine whatever may bring you joy. Are they things that you surround yourself with? Do you choose your actions, your thoughts, your relationships, and your occupation based upon what gives you joy? Or do you find yourself far from joy, forgetting that it is a choice, and believing that joy runs contradictory to productivity and success? Or, simply, that it is not available to *you?*

And most of us turn away from love just as we do joy. Everything comes back to the single choice we make. It was perhaps thrust upon us to begin with, yet we continue to make it, over and over again. What is it that allows this to continue unabated, so that suffering becomes the foundation of our lives?

Forgetting

From the beginning that is the breath, the journey continues through time and space, from beginning to end. There are levels beyond levels to this journey, but for each, it begins the same. No matter where you came from before, with no regard for the cycles that you have previously completed, the breath of God is the required act of being enlivened. Think of the doctor or midwife who pulls the baby from the mother's womb. She or he is the one who elicits the sound, who awakens the infant to what has transpired, acting as *an agent of the Divine.*

From this moment forward, there is either a community that receives the child and supports the connection with the light, with love—what we can call alignment and remembering—or the child is received into a situation where love does not exist, where it has been forgotten, neglected or is to be found only under layers of confusion, doubt, fear, and pain.

Sometimes this child is able to awaken in those closest what has been forgotten. This is an unusual child whose life force is carried by an old soul—one who is practiced in remembering.

The patterns of connection are intact and activated.

At other times, the child elects to forget, perhaps because there is a past debt to be paid or old patterns that were not completed. For those who have come into this time as "wayshowers," they may need to travel the path from knowing to forgetting to remembering. So they can identify the ways in which we make the choice. To recognize that we have the choice, even if we have forgotten so thoroughly that we do not believe it.

Personal Will and Surrendered Will

And now we can deepen the exploration of *personal will*, that element we were given with the breath of life. We have free will to determine how we will utilize this gift of light and life from the breath of God. We can *choose*.

In my early life, I felt cast out. Cast out of being loved and left alone without allies. Yes, I had free will; I had a choice. I could have turned inward to feel my connection that was never truly gone. But I was unable to do that. At least, I didn't do that. There was no outside support or modeling for that choice. In not experiencing love in my environment, my choice was framed by what I saw: *disconnection*.

Will is the capacity to make choices about what you want. It can also be the act of imposing your wants on a person or situation. To have willpower is to impose control over yourself. This may be to *do*, or to *not do* something.

With the Remembrance of your fundamental connection with *all that is*, you step into a whole new experience of will.

Being transparent to the Universal Field is being part of the whole of creation. You are permeable to Source. You act not from your agenda, nor your expectations. Instead, you allow what the Energies are here to do, what creation wishes to create.

To me, the word "surrender" works best here, but I do need to qualify it. Think of surrendering to Presence or surrendering to the bigger picture.

You are neither giving in nor giving up. When you surrender to Presence you are saying yes. Truly you are *living* a Yes. Yes, to receive. Yes, to the unknown. Yes, to the partnership of self with Self.

You are a creator! You are an integral part of whatever is being created, because without you acting upon the physical world, there is no manifestation. Yet, without your recognition of Source, without that which wishes to come through you, you can never express the full potency of what is possible.

In the old way of doing things, you strive to "manage" the creation. The problem with this is that as soon as your agenda runs the show, the show becomes an expression of your personal will. Collective co-creation stops. You can no longer "hear" the subtle voice.

You are no longer transparent to the Field.

When you allow yourself to be in co-creation, you are, in fact, exercising your *surrendered will*. You become permeable to Source. Your actions flow. Thoughts take form with ease. You recognize that you are needed *and* a part of this process, and that there is the bigger picture in motion. You are held and contained in something beyond your personal will.

When you surrender to that, you don't disappear, you don't disengage from the process. Rather, you become part of a new expression, part of what is being created in the moment. This is surrendered will in action.

This is exciting! You are actually the creator. And you don't do it by yourself. You don't *have* to do it by yourself. You have the support of this interconnected Field that you live in—and with which you get to express and create. So, in surrendering, you *affirm* your own creatorship as you express Divine Will.

Love and the Creative Life Force

Colm Kelleher, Ph.D., in *The Bak Journal*, eloquently says, "The creative capability of the human brain has lain in a dungeon, gathering cobwebs for millennia after millennia as mankind has sought a solution to its problems through ever more intense use of the intellect. When the heart opens and love or the creative life force is allowed to function beyond emotion, this stagnant circle is finally broken, and the brain and the heart join to make a new creative dance. The intellect is not abandoned when the heart opens; it simply moves into a different plane of operation.... When the intellect dominates our worldview, we only use a fraction of the capacity of our brains. When we live in our hearts, we begin to fully use our birthright."[4]

When your life is aligned, you are continually in a state of creating. Nothing is done by rote—not your choices nor your actions. You choose your thoughts and where to place your attention with awareness. Consider that your life is a creative process that has been designed to work.

When you pay attention to how your body feels, notice whether it feels restricted in any way, or if there is a feeling of freedom. Get to know the difference between a restricted body and a free body. When your body becomes free, you open the door for new creativity, fully immersing yourself in the flow of life.

Alignment

Imagine, if you will, receiving this breath of God, filling yourself with it, and recognizing that the gift is not a gift that comes because you have earned it. It's not something that is bestowed because of the special thing that you have done. It *is* because you are special. However, your specialness is because *you are who you are*. Here is the truth: there is nothing you

---

4 Colm Kelleher, Ph.D., *The Bak Journal*, August 1992, p. 3

can do to alter that. It is a matter of personal significance that this life has been granted to you. That you have been *enlivened* by God's breath.

So now that you are alive, how is it that you are to use this life force?

As a child, you undertake the necessary learning. There is your effort to grow, to receive guidance, to express what is true and unique about you.

When you allow yourself to receive the life force, you align with the Creative Intelligence of the Universe and can use it in the service of all that you create.

Choice

Choice is a part of the bargain, a part of the plan.

We are consciousness brought forth into the physical realm. Since everything has an energetic frequency, we can understand that this is where God brings a higher vibration into manifestation. Inherent in this manifestation is the aspect of choice, what some call free will. We forget so easily that we have the gift of choice. We forget that we came from Love. We ignore the love that we think is removed from us, not realizing that we can feel it within us at any moment—and in *every* moment. Love is forgotten as if it never existed. *Because when we try to feel our way into it, we do not know how.* So, we default to using the intellect that we have mirrored all around us.

We cannot feel this lost love because of the layers of separation that have been put into place. If those outside of us have no memory, and if we feel ourselves bound to them (they are our caregivers and wayshowers, after all), we do not know how to go against the power of the negative.

This, too, is a force, and it can be mighty. Some of us are drawn to the physical demonstration of this power. It is how "success" is portrayed. This may be played out in the realm of money, social or political attainment, or admiration from others. We aren't drawn to it because it brings joy. And certainly not because it feels good under the surface. Yet it becomes what we think we must strive for, not recognizing it as the path of separation from our true potential.

Love, Creativity, Inspiration, and Innovation

How do you find inspiration to create, to innovate, and bring something new into being?

I used to read a lot of texts, articles, and white papers about innovation. I have to admit that many times I fell asleep in the midst of reading and judged myself for it! I *should* be absorbing more, since this is my focus. I certainly shouldn't be falling asleep!

However, it's not enough to have a smart innovation theory. In both my consulting work and as a solutions engineer, I've known too many attempts at innovation that have short-circuited.

Teams falling apart. Communication breaking down.

Burnout before arrival at the finish line.

The wrong focus, with the adaptability and ability to shift nowhere in sight.

Here's why. Innovation cannot successfully happen by adopting a certain framework. Because content is not enough, even when it is great stuff.

The best tool is still only a tool.

YOU are what is needed. In your essence. With the vibration of love.

Is your own innovation intelligence optimized and operational? This includes an understanding and ease with the energetics of innovation. Of change. Of creativity. Of the relationship of your inner focus to your purpose.

Because when your purpose is clear, you align with what you are here to do and with the potential solution. You know how the roles of people, resources and timing fit together into a master plan.

Most importantly, the guidance and clarity from your inner connection will allow you to successfully navigate the continually shifting landscape and address the fears and concerns—of your teams and stakeholders or your family and friends.

The first step is to go inside. This might be through meditation. The art of connecting with the profound depths within you becomes something far more powerful than simple relaxation (although I don't diminish how needed this is, too). It becomes a vehicle to connect with your Creative Intelligence, the life force that uses whatever tools are in your arsenal to create exactly what is needed for that moment, and to do it with ease and flow.

Meditation will help you with a problem you want to solve. It can help bring your dreams to reality, bringing ideas into form.

I've been doing twice-weekly online Turaya Meditation© gatherings for over nine years and have been teaching meditation for almost thirty years. There are a host of reasons I could give you for "why meditate now, more than ever" (inner peace, resilience, better health, clarity, enhanced creativity).

Instead of investigating those further, let's look at meditation in the service of inspiration and innovation.

There have been hundreds of times in these group meditations where people have received clear guidance as to their next step in life, or for a project they are working on. They have "downloaded" detailed course content for a new offering, images of a painting to be created, solutions to family issues, even brand colors to be used in their marketing materials. Authors have dissolved blocks to their words, musicians for their compositions. Business owners have solved sticky communication problems.

Meditation brings you to the space between thoughts where you can then more easily tune into the elements in the field of potentiality that resonate with what you are wishing to create.

Your inner connection is where you find your footing and your inspiration.

Inside is where we connect with the truth of who we are. With the resources that are available to navigate clearly and with confidence. It is the source of our creative, resourceful response to anything and everything that comes our way. It is where innovation is born.

Yes: innovation, because we need new answers to what's happening, and they won't be found by doing the same things we've always done.

Be Inspired for Your Whole Life

A while back I interviewed renowned author and biologist, Rupert Sheldrake, for *Wisdom Talk Radio*. He said, "If you are going to believe that you can be inspired, you have to believe that there is something that can inspire you."

In the old mechanistic view of the universe, there was no greater consciousness to be accessed. It simply didn't exist. What you saw was what *was*; there was nothing more. With the most recent research in physics and the nature of the universe, we now know, and it has been demonstrated in countless experiments, that consciousness exists throughout nature—indeed, throughout the cosmos. It is the fundamental aspect: consciousness is energy.

Here is why that is so important.

When you are in relationship with the source of creation, the Universal Field of potential, then you have something from which to be inspired.

How do you access this relationship consistently and reliably? Inspiration is, quite literally, the act of breathing in. What if you could breathe in from the consciousness of higher intelligence? Since this intelligence is the Universal Field of energy of which you are a part, then you can receive answers that are beyond your what-you-see-is-what-you-get level of consciousness. These answers are often perceived as strange by your mental mind, or "beyond" your normal state. But once you integrate them, you can bring these ideas into form as the answer to what was needed, or as the creation to be born.

Laurie Seymour

Think of what your life would be like if you could be inspired at every moment. With each breath that you take, you feel the resonance of connection. You feel the flow of life itself coursing through you.

Inspiration is the act of co-creation. You are co-creating with the Universe. In your human self, *you* are the one who must act. This is the crucial element in the whole innovation and creation process.

The Source of your inspiration cannot act upon the world. Only you can do that. So, if you sit and wait for inspiration to strike, and then do nothing with it when it does, then *you aren't doing your part in the co-creation equation.*

Going within. Inspiration. Action. Each element is required for innovation and creation.

You can move through life in this state of co-creation, so that you live inspired. When you "forget," you can "remember" with your very next breath.

This is where things like meditation take their place: in the service of your co-creating. In getting quiet, in learning how to listen within, you drop into relationship and communication with Source.

This is what I learned with Dawn: how to live life as it is meant to be lived. As it can be lived!

Collective Co-Creation

As part of the Quantum Connection Process that I created with The Baca Institute, I saw a need for a program to support conscious entrepreneurs, innovators, and visionary leaders to be able to bring their ideas to fruition. Time after time, I saw these leaders get stuck. They would have an inspired idea. They got excited by its potential for transformation. But then they would forget the Source of that idea, turning instead to the isolated structures that they typically relied on to function in the world. They didn't know how to use their Creative Intelligence! They would burn out or get mired in self-doubt and feel overwhelmed.

When you are creating something new, it is difficult to stay connected with the energy of what is knocking on your door!

The Quantum Co-Creation Program was born. I brought a small group of people together for six months, focused on both internal co-creation, which arises in Remembrance, and co-creation (beyond mere collaboration) with others. When two or more are gathered in the Remembrance of their connection with Source, an exponentiation of the energy is activated. It is as if your cohesion with Source invites others into a profound collaboration with you.

This is what I discovered: creative expression and transformation are not linear, and neither is your journey of bringing your idea to life. It moves the most expansively and can accelerate in leaps and bounds when you are connected to other conscious entrepreneurs on a similar path. Even when you put systems in place to make your idea physical, or bring others into your project, this is done with greater ease and clarity when you are guided through your connection with Source. When you create within a group in which each is dedicated to remembering who they are, the collaborative ideas flow from the synergy of inner knowing.

I imagine you have experienced meetings where, while the purpose was to innovate something, they devolved into ego-fenced silos, and little was accomplished. If you are lucky, you have also had the pleasure of spontaneous collective co-creation.

Maybe you worked with a team to enhance the quality of a program or product. Or you met with a potential collaborator to create something to offer to the public. Perhaps you gathered stakeholders for a high-stakes conversation to bring a vision into form: one with far-reaching implications for solving a thorny problem.

It is common for each person to enter a meeting like this with an agenda. They have the "best" idea. They know the "right" steps to take. With this certainty, they neither know how to access something new from within themselves, nor how to truly listen to someone else's ideas. They don't know how to discern the difference between an ego agenda and an inspired idea.

But no one can get to someplace new by doing things the way they have always done them!

You can, however, intentionally set the stage for co-creation.

To create a collective co-creation space, each member needs to be in a state of focused relaxation. Once your thoughts slow down, you can access greater clarity and even discover fresh solutions.

As you become practiced in holding "open space" within yourself, you may notice ideas bubbling to the surface. Open space is needed before you create action lists, and certainly before details are fleshed out. The ideas that arise out of open space may come in the form of pictures or in seemingly unrelated ideas. You may notice physical sensations like heat or the movement of energy, or you may feel stirred up. These physical sensations are often an activation of new aspects of yourself. They are an indication that there is something more to pay attention to. This is the time to go deeper within yourself. Don't push. Don't rush it. Allow.

So, begin the gathering with a period of quiet, inner focus, inviting open space. This shifts you from the daily tasks that had claimed your attention to a field where something new can arise. Hold an intention for something to emerge in your time together. Hold it lightly, without being attached to how it will look, what will emerge, and especially, to the results. When each of you becomes practiced on staying with your own connection to Source, then your team enters into a collective co-creation experience. The process isn't linear. You have moved into the realm where quantum leaps take place. That is, where potential manifests into form without necessarily knowing the route. It is a whole-system process, fueled by the unlimited potential of the Universal Field. This is more than working in flow. You bring the potency of Source.

One experience of collective co-creation happened in meeting Yvonne Dam, at that time a new friend and colleague living in Barcelona, Spain. Our work is quite different. Yet during our initial Zoom conversations, we each had a sense that there was something for us to create together. There was a vibrancy and a kind of quiet excitement that spoke of something that was worthy of exploration.

I had a walking trip planned in the Cotswolds, in the UK. It seemed like the most natural thing in the world to extend that trip with a short hop to Spain. Yvonne graciously invited me to stay with her and her family.

The Moreness Retreat emerged from this time of collective co-creation. We visited potential retreat centers, marveling at how our senses were attuned to what did and didn't align with the energy of our vision. We gathered a support team for the retreat that resonated with the vision.

The retreat week itself was a flow of Unconditional Love. We all, participants and staff alike, experienced profound and lasting transformations. Coming together, Yvonne and I created something that was far more than just a joint offering. We took quantum leaps together that facilitated the same in the participants. The alchemy of co-creation took us into more "Moreness" than we could have imagined. We witnessed participants having an internal experience of abundance. Whatever was next, the inner connection was dependable. Even our chef was inspired to make a major shift in her business!

36

The Primary Relationship

I feel myself in an altered state. This is a state of Remembrance. It is filled with realizations upon realizations. The moment has come to embrace even more deeply where this is going.

 This is the path that you have chosen for this book. It has chosen you and you have chosen it. It works both ways. In truth, it is your heart's desire.

Let's talk a little more about the power of love. Not love in the abstract or in the emotional—emotional love takes its toll on you; it doesn't nourish the cells. It sends you up to the top of one hill and down into another pit. There is no ground or grounding. But when you feel the fullness of Unconditional Love overflowing within you, then you realize that this vibration of love takes you to a place and a power that does not exist elsewhere.

So, let's put the old concept of love to bed. Ignore the songs and the poems that speak of romantic love. Not that there is anything to struggle against in that. Of course, it may even be the avenue through which you come to realize the bigger picture that is possible. But so often we get so caught up in measuring and comparing—as in *who loves who more* and *does he/she love me truly?* —that we forget what is possible and ignore what is real.

The vibration of Unconditional Love can come alive in relationships. There, it can be the foundation upon which you create a way of living that feels *truer*.

With the realization of the *inner* primary relationship, with a Remembrance of the love from which you came, you can put into place a foundation of truth in your personal relationships. It only takes one within the relationship to remember and to hold that vibration. That vibration acts to remind and recover the Remembrance of the original connection. It helps the other to recover their own Remembrance. This creates a unique opportunity to work within the system of any relationship, whether it is romantic partners, parent/child or employer/employee.

In the eighties, I taught a seminar called The Nature of Love in Management for the Oregon Zoo in Portland. I was exploring the impact of love on an organizational team where their manager held and led with an understanding and acknowledgment of her own inner connection. I saw that living from an awareness of her connection brought a rich ground of Unconditional Love that fostered communication and innovation. Her team's capacity expanded to create innovative display solutions while working within budget constraints. Concurrently, the team's reported job satisfaction levels rose dramatically.

The nature of love in management centers on the recognition of the uniqueness of each person. It has to do with recognizing the true nature of each person's divinity, so that they can be that light for others. In fact, it's not important whether this happens from the top down or the bottom up, whether the person is the CEO, a manager, or an individual contributor. The only thing that matters is the vibrational shift (elevation of frequency) that takes place in the team with a conscious, aware person in the mix.

Each organization has its own Creative Intelligence. In order to tap into the highest level of performance, the power of collective genius becomes available when each team member comes from the field of Unconditional Love. Then they step into their unique strengths, talents, and capabilities as they relate to Creative Intelligence, the connection with the Field.

As a trainer, as part of teams, as a consultant to teams, as a leader of teams, I've had countless experiences of this power of love in groups. It's never necessary to speak about love (that would, after all, be merely "talking about," and not a direct experience). But it is certainly what people experience when they feel honored and acknowledged for their own unique being. They are able to contribute to the whole from the essence of who they are. This connection with themselves and their creative essence is mirrored in their connection with the team. This is what fuels true innovation and co-creation.

Our Original Blueprint

What happens when a conscious person enters into any relational system, be it an organization, a team, a family, or a couple?

There are those of us who were with Dawn for years. And there are other "Dawns," as she always said. She was not the only one. The Ascended ones are ever-present, bringing into the light those who would lead by way of teaching by example, and most importantly, in energy. The act of Initiation is an act of recovering what was lost. It is a quantum leap forward made possible by the reclaiming of what was always in place but forgotten. This is the activation. This is the role that we, in our human form, are here to play. We are the activators—of ourselves and of those around us.

This works because we are given everything we need...only we don't know it. Or our personal will is so strong that we diminish the opportunities to step forth and become leaders in our own lives.

I use the term *leaders* broadly here. You may not be the person in charge or running the show. Instead, think of a leader as a guide or instigator. To instigate something, you move people to act. To instigate and to activate are related. In order to activate someone, you awaken or turn on the system that will allow them to become who they are meant to be.

This "system" is the original blueprint within the human cell that is activated.

We come into this world as perfect beings. We come with the opportunity to *act* from within or to *react* to the outer world. If our outer life situation provides us the "opportunity" to forget, maybe that's because there are aspects that must be added to the blueprint so that we can become who we are here to be.

This is how I have come to understand and appreciate the trajectory of my own life.

The purpose of a particular situation or event may never be discovered. Let's assume that there *is* a reason, even if we don't know what it is. We know it isn't a bad reason, or a punishment: the truth is that it is never about punishment.

In fact, it is always about becoming more conscious.

So, what does it mean to become conscious? I have come to take my place amongst those who are ready to lead.

What matters is that I am here to activate because I have first activated myself. I have received the Energies of initiation and have surrendered my will to God's will. In doing this, I have received far more than anything that you might imagine that I have given up.

In fact, I have given up nothing, because there was nothing but struggle in that way of being. I gladly release the suffering. I wholeheartedly wish to claim my purpose for coming here: my original blueprint. This opens the way for what I bring to others.

We have the actions of forgetting and remembering. We have the activation of this Remembrance. We have Inner Law that help us to maintain the Remembrance—the vibration of Unconditional Love. What is missing here is the part that I see with my client Luke, who knows all of this and yet frequently gives in to struggle and suffering. He is one of the most self-aware people I know, but has difficulty navigating his place in the world. He often imagines himself judged by others. In the midst of struggle, he has a moment of feeling love, activated as he feels the Energies, and he is back in the flow. He remembers what is true.

He forgets, but not because the Energies abandon him.

Life tests us.

These situations bring to our conscious awareness where we are in relation to the bigger picture. They show us our patterns so that we can see them, instead of being stuck on repeat, caught in unawareness. They point us to where our thoughts have drifted and where the flow has stopped.

In these moments, you have the opportunity to shift your thinking so that the feeling of love in your body can be reclaimed.

The first step is the realization that your thoughts may not be the truth about either you or the situation but have arisen out of a turning away from this ever-present field of love. How do you stop being so pig-headed that you decide that your current thoughts must be the truth, simply because you think them! Because the next thought on that particular path is that your previous feelings of flow and love are to be dismissed as bunk.

This attitude will only cause you more suffering. Everything that you doubt reflects what you long to have. I always wanted to feel loved and valued. Yet, anytime I felt that, I had self-doubt at the ready, standing by to crush the incipient light before it had a chance to grow into a blazing sun.

Instead, if you turn towards the feeling that supports you—the feeling that makes you glow from within—then you will see that this is a very different way to be in the world.

There will always be opportunities to forget the true essence of who you are. To ignore it. This is the nature of life. Not only to test you, but to teach whatever you need to learn. It is how you raise your consciousness. Some would say that you chose the particular situation for your growth before you were born (see Michael Newton, *Journey of Souls*).

In life, you are presented with situations that offer you the possibility for growth. It is the choice that comes before you in each moment. Which will it be? The darkness or the light?

It is easy to recognize people who do damage to others. In countless ways, people diminish others' right to live and to express themselves. You do to others what you do to yourself.

For any of this to change, you must start in your own house, with the damage you do to yourself by forgetting the truth.

How can you do it differently? Right now, at this moment.

People came to me over the years that I was in private practice as a psychotherapist, wanting something different in their lives. Too often, though, what they really wanted was permission to stay the way that they were. They wanted justification for feeling miserable.

The Energies that are here to love you will not allow this to continue. There is a rigor to this way of being. There is nothing "soft" about it. The rigor of the Energies wants you to be in this state-in-motion of Unconditional Love. As soon as you are in the vibration of Unconditional Love, you realize the untruth of the previous moment when you were filled with self-doubt.

Because self-doubt cannot stand with love. The power and the truth of love is on a different plane. So, when you are resonating *there*, the rest no longer exists. And as you stay with this vibration, you recognize that it shifts and changes. It continually expands into something new that you would never be able to recognize from the old dimension.

This is the way that consciousness grows. You might have thought of consciousness as something *formed*, static, because that is how your human self tries to make sense of it. But stasis cannot exist with Unconditional Love. Consciousness, by its nature, never stops and never goes back. There is only forward motion and *centropy*. The other side of this dance is *entropy*, a decline into disorder and chaos, which shuts down consciousness. To be centropic, you must come to a place of embracing all that is, knowing that you can turn your attention and shift what you feel in the body.

The first step in shifting your attention is to become curious. Where do your thoughts take you? What is the nature of your thoughts? How do your attitudes about life (and everything else) flavor what you focus on?

You can be playful with what you discover.

Seriousness has killed many a potentially conscious moment. Playfulness, on the other hand, opens you to engaging with these elements rather than locking them in chains. Oh, I feel like hitting my kid because they're mouthing off to me? Wow, where did that come from? I can't stand how my husband is washing the dishes? Ah, okay, I see that the judge is ready for action!

In each moment, there is the opportunity for curiosity and play. An opportunity for a different way of embracing the moment. And in all of this is the theme of inner inquiry, a.k.a. Inner Research.

Inner Research

Inner Research is the act of turning inward to discover more about yourself. When you look at your actions, your behavior, your thoughts, as things you need to explore instead of as something that needs to be fixed, suddenly you have space in which to look at them without rancor. There needs to be no judgment, either, so that you can look with love on that hurt child that was you, the scared teenager, the fearful adult.

There is an aspect of you that can "witness" all of this from the perspective of a compassionate and loving being. Even if that part of you feels completely buried, there is always something of the original spark of Divine connection that is alive and can be brought to the present moment.

Each time you allow this part of you to surface, it becomes stronger. The path of accessing this witness part of you becomes channeled within you as a new pathway that allows you to connect with the inner teacher/parent/God presence.

Discovery of your capacity to be a witness is the first step in a new way of being with you. I feel the witness always is a part of me, and yet somehow not of my personality. It is neutral, as an observer would be. There is no emotional charge. The witness isn't *reactive*.

The beauty is that it is the vibration of Unconditional Love. When that part of me is running the show, and I can step into its frequency, I am enveloped by grace. I feel released from the clutches of old emotional reactions.

There must be something on which to focus one's mental attention so that what happens during the initiations can be received without interference. Quiet and activity go hand in hand. The activity of the mind can be focused on understanding and reviewing one's actions. The art of Inner Research can become the means by which one keeps occupied while the Energies do their work. The cellular transformation can then unfold uninhibited.

While Inner Research serves to occupy the mind so that the Energies can do what is needed in the physical body with all of its habits and patterns, there is another dimension that becomes evident. When you actively undertake Inner Research, you acknowledge that you are willing to set aside judgment, to become curious instead, to explore and untangle the web of inner deception that you had adopted.

It is an activation process in and of itself.

Here is another way to consider this. The seed of *knowing* exists—of Remembrance of the truth—with or without your direct awareness of it. When you open your intention to examine your thoughts, your patterns, and attitudes, you effectively state to the Universe that you are willing to recover and remember.

You are looking for what is true about your existence, not for an old story.

All of your current stories have the potential to lead you to the well. Whether you drink from this well or a different one, you have come to a place of choice. So, recognizing that you have made a choice means that you have greater awareness in play.

Awareness is an activator.

This is a critical point. It is why awareness is so important. And it's why there are so many books and courses that teach you to be more self-aware. But awareness alone is not enough. Awareness can get old and stale. You can become patterned in your awareness. Because the juiciness that you are seeking, the nectar that will fill your being, comes from your inner experience of love. It comes from that primary relationship of self with Self, whose source is inside you. When this inner relationship is thriving—that is, when you live fully the truth of your Remembrance, then your relationship with someone else can become an extension and reflection of this inner one.

Too often relationships are blurry facsimiles of the dismembered portions of your inner relationship. In this inner relationship, you have something that goes beyond the trinity of Father/Son/Holy Spirit created by the early church, 300 years after the death of Jesus. In Matthew, 28:16, *Christian Standard Bible*, Jesus instructed the apostles: "Go therefore and make disciples of all nations, baptizing them in the name of the Father and of the Son and of the Holy Spirit."

That trinity could be understood and experienced in a different way. It needs an updating to embrace the full experience of the sacred. Consider Mother/Father/Teacher. These three are the aspects of God that are represented by what I call the Inner Teacher. Our personal, direct relationship with God is with the Inner Teacher.

To be filled with the Holy Spirit as Matthew uses it, is to be filled with the Remembrance of you and God being one. This Remembrance can be rediscovered (remembered) through the energetic openings (we could call them blessings) that you experience in life.

God is the essence, the "beingness." The Mother and the Father are the roles (persons) through which we interact with or get to know the essence. The essence of Unconditional Love is the same expression of God through different vehicles. The Inner Teacher is the inner personal experience of the essence of the spirit of God, which was called the Holy Spirit. Guidance comes from this spirit.

There is so much that has been kept from us. Recorded history is not what is true. Partial truth is not truth. How many times have you looked back on your personal history and realized that what you thought you knew wasn't the complete picture? It is the same when competing interests obscure the real story. When those who have external power wish to hold onto and solidify their power, the truth is often the first thing to go.

When the "party line" creates separation (us and them), it demands that we forget the truth. With separation comes fear, lack, and rage, which become the currency of control. We need only look to the experience of Jesus at the hands of those who wished only to remain in power, to see this in full expression. This has been mirrored in civilization after civilization.

Then we have Mary Magdelene who was powerful in her own right. The incredible research done by Kathleen McGowan and others into her true history gives us the opportunity to remember what was forgotten: Mary was the "disciple to the disciples." She was a great teacher with her own expression in the world. She was absolutely dedicated to teaching the Way of Love and persisted despite judgment and condemnation.

This was forgotten because it was hidden. It was hidden because the levers of control were manipulated by those who thought they would, in some way, lose what they had: position, power, wealth. Love was never the guiding force.

For Mary, though, the center of everything was Love. It was the fullness of remembering who we are.

Love is at the center of remembering.

I feel so blessed that in *remembering*, I have claimed a new relationship with my father. That throughline continued into my relationship with Dawn, experiencing the two archetypal essences, male and female, that returned me to the Remembrance of my own essence. This impacted relationships with both of my parents. It wasn't only with my father. It allowed me to find a new relationship with my mother, as well, so that my heart could receive her love.

Our outer world experiences may or may not be ones that are to be cherished as nurturing. And when they are not, it becomes ever more difficult (and even more essential) to remember our original connection with Source. What often happens is that the mirror gets mistaken for reality. Then, if the mirror is distorted in any way (as it so often is), reality is put to the test, usually leaving self-doubt in its wake. *Is love truly available to me? Am I loveable? Am I "worthy" of being loved?*

We Don't Need to Be Saved, We Need to Remember

It is remarkable to see the control that formalized religion exercises in its domination of thought. It shows up most directly in the "requirement" for intercessors between you and God. This has meant that you are constantly reminded that there is no direct connection available for you with God. Compounding this are the distorted mirrors that are provided to us in the form of all-too-human priests, ministers, and rabbis.

Where do we find love? Certainly, *never in the same place where there is control.*

This is the original sin if something like that even exists. That we are in Plato's cave, where we mistake the reflection for the real thing. This sets us up for relationships to begin and to end, bitterly, after we discover that this reflection was no better than the one before. Parents are set up to be larger than life, idols, only to be found to have clay feet when we, as children, think they are to be our gods. The same thing happens in adult relationships, whether that is with a love partner, a teacher, or a boss.

The refrain of "look within, look within" grows ever louder. There is no warmth from the fire's reflection (although you may be very good at imagining it to be there). The real thing is only there when you sit before the source, *in relationship with its sustaining heat.*

I spent years being attracted to predatory men, merging two of the elements that seemed most promising as a source of love: teacher and father. Because I was vulnerable in my looking outwards to find the source of love, sex seemed like a good facsimile. At least it brought a degree of closeness and connection. Except that so often there was no real connection. I prided myself on not being a victim: that I willingly entered into these "relationships."

I didn't realize that what I really wanted couldn't be found in those places. I never found it. And so often I felt the yuck of what I had stepped into. Believe me, more is not better. It would have been better to focus on my relationships with my peers, whether they were satisfying or not. But they just didn't get close to the possibility of father/teacher—that portion of the triad that I believed held what I was missing.

Perhaps it is fair to say that we can have any relationship and have it be satisfying, as long as we don't layer on top of it the desire for Mother/Father/Teacher. Because that's when things become troublesome. We create suffering for ourselves because the aspect we desire is missing and then we become judgmental of our partner because of this lack!

Think about it. The incredible weight that must be borne by the man or woman that we say we are in love with. We are in love with the ghost of our *memory* of love (the reflection of the fire), the hazy memory of the expression of Source.

We are truly longing for this. We truly want to love and be loved. We just look for it in the wrong place. We expect it to be something that the storybooks tell us about. We never think to look inside.

Why would we look inside? Everything in the world says we find love with another. The books, movies, poems, plays, songs: they all tell us tales of undying love, or of love gone wrong, or of being done wrong. Then there are the stories of the men or women who have stayed apart from life and dedicated themselves to God. The nuns who marry Jesus and wear a wedding ring. The monks and hermits who inhabited the solitary caves I saw in Turkey.

This doesn't suit most of us, however. It's not the path that will bring us the joy that we have an inkling is possible.

Permission to look inside to meet this longing is rarely to be found in the outer world. So, we seek the perfect partner. TV shows mirror the search and the difficulties inherent in the search. Ah true love, where do you live? It seems harder and harder to find it in the places we look.

Yes, there are plenty of successful, happy partnerships. Love is part of that, of course. Perhaps they are successful in that neither partner expects the other to be Mother/ Father/ Teacher. If we do not find it in outer world relationships, where then? How is it that we are to find this union if not in our outer relationships? Because in fact, it is a union.

Sometimes, there appears in life someone like Dawn was for me. A loving teacher who could mirror my own divinity. Someone who had no need to be my guru. A true master who taught each of us who came to be with her to be masters of our own self. This relationship provided me with the means to experience for myself the Inner Teacher. She taught us to listen—not to her, but to our own inner voice. She taught us discernment, so that we could feel the difference between the words of the inner teacher and the desires of ego. This, for me, was like gold because it went to the heart of my self-doubt. My self-doubt, remember, was rooted in the space between what I had experienced and knew to be true and what I had forgotten and what felt lost in the mist.

Being able to discern the source of my inner direction gave me the means to relax into trusting my own guidance. I didn't have to rely on an outer world teacher, therapist, priest, or guru. You cannot be sufficient unto yourself without this discernment. You cannot find the strength to claim yourself and what brings you joy as long as someone else holds the keys to your truth.

This is what is possible. This is what the inner journey is about and why it is worthwhile beyond belief.

The Inner Journey

The inner journey is not taken to fix what is broken in you (although we may think that is the case). As I have said before, you aren't broken at all. Religion brings the need of repentance in order to find God's grace. However, Jim Palmer, founder of The Center for Non-Religious Spirituality, says this about repentance:

> The word "repent" (metanoia—the original Greek) means a deep and profound shift in perception. It's a turning about in the deepest seat of our consciousness or awareness. It's like the blinders fall off, and we see things as they really are. Metanoia literally means "beyond the mind." It's seeing and perceiving from within our innermost self.[5]

We go beyond what had been keeping us from our own truth. We *remember*.

Reflection

What is driving you?

What moves you from one place to another?

Do you know what you want?

5 Jim Palmer, "One of the worst explained verses in the Bible is Matthew 3:2: 'Repent, for the kingdom of heaven is at hand.'"0/, Inner Anarchy, Divine Nobody Press, Facebook, January 26, 2024, http://bit.ly/40TSrQI

> If you know, are you moving towards it? Do you
> give yourself permission to do that?

The inner journey is parallel to the outer journey. They are not separate. In fact, each informs the other. What you allow for yourself in your life opens you to a deeper relationship with Self. Life is not a journey of self-abnegation. Nor suffering. It is a journey of abundance.

This is where my growing edge lives. I stayed in the belief pattern of subsistence living for so long, even when my current husband and I were making multiple six figures. It's what I saw growing up. Even my brother, who has enough money to do whatever he wants in life, treats himself in a way that looks like suffering. He travels when and where he wants, but always with constraints that speak of self-neglect.

It is helpful to state what you want in your life. What I want now is the freedom to live where and how I want. To be surrounded by peace, by beauty, by love. I want the ability to explore what is possible. To live in places where I can absorb the vibrations of the culture and places that my being asks to receive. And where I carry forward the merger of inside and outside that is needed now.

This is not a message that can always be carried in words. It is shared in vibration. So, I can be in many different places, all around the globe, where just my presence can remind others of what lies hidden within them. I cannot do this only in words. That is the point. Sometimes people come to my events merely to have an experience. For them, it is enough to be reminded.

41

Abundance Is Love

If you are not experiencing abundance in your life, it is a direct reflection of feeling a lack of love. Lack is only about forgetting, remember? So, it follows that the key to shifting this experience of scarcity is to surrender to love. To breathe it in. Again and again.

I feel it. I feel it release the knots in my back. I feel a flow of cool energy through my body. This feeling of love brings me a picture of a verdant garden, filled with orchids and tropical plants. It is lush with growth.

Exercise Your Imagination

Imagine whatever abundance is to you. Breathe. Breathe and feel your breath as love. It's your connection to the original breath of God. Relish it. It is yours. It is why you are you. Then allow a picture to come to your mind's eye: something that comes from this feeling that the breath brings to you. Look at the details, the color, and the shapes. Notice any fragrance. Now take another breath and breathe into this picture so that it begins to glow. Let the light penetrate every portion of it. If there is a person in your picture, let the light fill that person. Notice how you feel as you gaze into this picture. Breathe into it and then breathe it into you until you are one with this picture.

It is helpful to anchor this picture. Let a number come to mind. This number represents, for you, this picture and this feeling of abundance. The number will anchor this as a feeling into your memory. You need only think of the number to fill you with a feeling of abundance. Do this now. Speak your number inside of you. Let it immediately bring this feeling to you, letting it fill your body head to toe, in every cell.

This is the opening to a new way of living. It is a new way of bringing Remembrance into physical expression. Life will continue to give you feedback. That's the thing. You don't have to wonder. You need only look at what shows up in your life. Receive it. It is yours.

Let me add a word of caution. It may be all too easy for you to decide that any outer world lack is because you have done something wrong. That you are not trying in the right way, not doing the right things, not thinking correctly.

Nope.

There are certainly things that aren't helpful and don't support where you are trying to go. It's simply that all of those old ways of thinking are the judgment that will only take you deeper into the fog of separation. So, you may be saying, "Yes, but if I'm doing something wrong, I want to change it. I want to do what's right."

I understand that. But instead of bringing in a feeling of lightness into your world, it's the same old judgment that comes scurrying forth.

I know this all too well. I can judge myself with both hands tied behind my back. And I'm equally good at judging others, mostly by deciding that they aren't doing things the way that I think they should. So, I am particularly careful with the judgment beast. It can bite you with no warning whatsoever. And it can disguise itself admirably in things that seem like caring, like concern.

Concern Is Not Caring

Concern so often masquerades as care. It's a form of civilized worry, dressed up to look good and be acceptable. "I'm concerned about how you are taking care of yourself." (*Translated*: I want you to treat yourself in some way other than you are, because you aren't doing things the way that I think is right.) "I'm concerned about what's happening in the world." (*Translated*: I don't like the events that are taking place, and somebody should do something about this!)

When you invest in a specific outcome, that outcome becomes your focus of concern. Judgment then disguises itself as concern.

It works like this. You have an expectation or agenda that something should be different. You want something to be done your way. The situation is not meeting your expectations about life.

Here's the thing about agendas or expectations that doesn't work.

Everyone is responsible for their own growth. Your idea of what is needed for someone else's own good is an infringement that thwarts everyone's freedom, yours and theirs.

First, you deny them freedom of self-discovery.

Then, realize that your own freedom depends upon your moment-to-moment awareness. When you feel concerned, you abandon self-awareness and deny yourself freedom to focus. You block the dynamic movement on your own path.

Why is this important? Because these blocks have consequences for your well-being. Judgment, concern, and manipulation all constrict you, limiting your ability to listen and to respond. Just imagine how many of your current thoughts create tightness in your body!

What if you dropped your expectations and concerns?

There is so much waiting for you on the other side. Your thoughts and pictures are vehicles for interaction with the world. Being present allows you to be a witness to life's situations while still maintaining your focus. With your thoughts free of concern, your clarity of awareness facilitates the dialogue between the outer environment and your inner guidance.

Your responsibility is to keep your inner compass pointed to true north—to the place inside that shows you the way forward and always resonates as truth. This is where your freedom lies.

Using life's feedback to judge yourself will only compound itself. Judgment breeds more judgment until you are in a doghouse of your own making.

I assume that if you are here, reading this book, that the doghouse is only for your beloved hound, and not for you. Let me invite you to get out of there.

Here is where Inner Research can become your best friend, your go-to way of working with the feedback that life brings.

When Something in Your Life is Not Flowing

When something in your life is not flowing, pay attention. Stop and notice what's going on. How do you describe it to yourself? How would you talk about it to someone else? Notice the tone that you use and the words that you choose. Be aware of how you feel as the speaker and what comes up as the listener. Are you mean or critical? Do you play the victim or hapless intruder?

Do any of these actually have any true power?

Is there real strength in them, or is there only drama and victimhood? Do you feel inclined to blame someone else for what is happening?

Your answers provide you with good clues. It may take you some time to unravel this: to find the truth of the situation. Is this familiar? Is it a pattern that you have repeated over and over again? This too isn't the opportunity to jump into judgment. Remember, you are the researcher who wants only to get back to the truth. Because you know that suffering isn't it.

Here is your operating assumption. You begin from the place where you state your hypothesis (remember high school chemistry?) and then test it. I begin with the hypothesis that when something is not flowing in my life, it is because I have stepped out of love—that I have stepped into a false story about myself, or about life.

It's an old pattern. A pattern is nothing more than a coagulation of stuck energy. You don't need to go to its roots to dissolve it. Although you may become aware of its historical source, you don't have to travel back in time to address it. Because at its foundation, it is simply energy, so you can attend to it vibrationally.

How? The key to dissolving the pattern becomes your experience of love. You return to where you began. You remember into the truth of life itself, which is always of love, always of connection.

This is how the feeling of love works to transform without incision. Love activates your Remembrance of truth.

Julie arrived for the Turaya Meditation© session feeling frustrated and out of sorts. Her face was pale, and her body looked constricted and uncomfortable. After twenty minutes of the meditation session, her whole being transformed as she experienced the energy through the transmissions. It was the difference between night and day. Her skin looked almost translucent. Her face had softened and radiated light.

She had remembered love.

Love has no need of understanding nor of figuring it out. In fact, as a chief "figure outer," I can tell you that this action does not bring you freedom. It may take you to a deeper understanding, but it's still limited by its linearity. Mental body be damned; it is not the way to truth. As someone with a highly developed and cherished mental body, I know that it can also provoke more trouble (especially in the realm of self-doubt) than satisfaction. Certainly, it does not bring the experience of truth.

So, let's go for something different, something that has the possibility to create a feeling of freedom in your body.

Feeling Freedom

Take a breath. As you breathe in, do you notice that your chest and maybe your belly expand as you take in the air? There is a physical expansion that happens when you inhale. In order to create space for your breath, your ribcage expands. Your body moves in harmony with the movement of your breath. There is simplicity and familiarity in this. As you soften, you begin to feel what truth is like in your body.

You can also think of being in the presence of someone who is calm and loving. Without even trying, your breath begins to slow. You calibrate yourself to them, resonating with this new frequency so that your frequency can shift.

Inner guidance is like this. At the cellular level, you seek the highest resonant field to vibrate with. The Universe responds. It amplifies the signals that you send.

When your inner world is noisy, that is, cluttered with to-do lists, worry, or judgment—the noise is magnified. You feel discomfort.

As you connect into the resonant field of potentiality, your own system attunes to what is possible. You *naturally* want to remember your place in the grand scheme, as a piece of the creative expression of the Universe. You become receptive to ideas and opportunities outside of your previous frame of reference.

When you quiet the noise so that clear signals can come through, you calibrate yourself to the new frequency. You feel inspired. Your questions are answered. You feel guided.

43

Laying Claim to Myself

What follows is a profound experience of my own coming to truth, previously published in the chapter "Laying Claim to Myself," in *The Wisdom of Midlife Women 2*.

I thought I could do it. I thought I could stay in my marriage with Sid even though my heart felt like it was caught in mud. My relationship with my seven-year-old daughter felt out of whack. I kept retreating from something that stayed clouded in my vision. That I was unhappy was clear to me. I just didn't know what to *do* about it. So, I barely acknowledged my desperation even within the privacy of my own thoughts.

I'd learned so thoroughly to live from the outside-in regarding my marriage. Through our twenty-some years of being married, friends and family often told us what a great couple we were. When I was a psychotherapist, my practice included clients with troubled marriages that I helped bring to clarity. Still, I had packed up the slippery questions about the viability of my own marriage and trundled them away.

Then my husband was diagnosed with cancer. I felt this deep love welling up that seemed to sweep away my growing realization of how weighed down I felt. It helped me hang in.

That feeling of connection didn't last.

My husband came through all of his treatments successfully: two rounds of chemo, then surgery, followed by weeks of radiation making it nearly impossible for him to swallow. Through all of the treatments, we had faced the real possibility of his death. The rawness of this time shredded the cultivated image that we had held onto for so long. Aching truths about our relationship surfaced.

The not-so-funny joke among our friends was that I was the controller, and he was the good guy. The truth is, when a good guy goes along with a controller, there's a lot of anger. When a controller hangs out with a good guy, you can be sure there's a passel of control going on underneath the surface of the good guy. My control was overt; his control was passive. It ran deep into the heart of our relationship. I was looking to be loved. He was looking to make sure he wouldn't be left.

I realized I had believed in his image of what a good mother looked like (his mother), invalidating my own expression as a mother. Since he was the "loving" parent, energetically, I stayed off to the side.

Acknowledging the truth allowed me to breathe into the new space that opened inside of me. I faced this unequivocal realization: I could no longer continue in my marriage. This came side by side with fear of the opinion I thought my friends and family would have of me if I left. *My husband had come through cancer!* How could I leave him?

I didn't act. But I couldn't "*unsee*" what now seemed so obvious. With the veil of my self-deception lying in tatters, the soul-robbing trade-offs we had established to keep our marriage intact stood bare. We had spent years creating false stories of ourselves and our relationship, colluding to stay together. The cost was skyscraper high. I was no longer willing to pay that price.

What was I willing to give up in order to find what was true?

By that time in my life, I had been building a relationship with my own inner voice for a long time. It was something I had learned to trust to help me navigate my life.

My husband and I had just set out for a walk in our neighborhood. My body felt tight; I noticed energy began to move strongly in me, vibrating, making it difficult to breathe.

I knew I had to pay attention to what was happening.

"I have to go. I can't stay in this marriage any longer. I can't do it."

That was *my* voice saying that. I hadn't decided to speak at that moment. I had simply *allowed* myself to speak. It happened before I could even think about what I was doing. But as soon as I said those words there was such a rush of feeling in my body. It felt completely and utterly true.

There wasn't any doubt in me, no holdbacks to counter what I had just declared.

I was no longer willing to give up *myself*. In order to claim my own life, to live from the inside-out instead of from the outside-in, I stopped buying into trade-offs and illusion. We had spent so many years with our eyes closed and our voices muted that we were confusing soul-enhancement with safety. What a trap safety turned out to be!

For a while, it was difficult to believe I had been so unwilling to see the truth. It was completely counter to my self-image! I had to face disappointing those who mistook the surface equanimity of our relationship for the whole picture. I could no longer act based on what others would think or who I would upset. Instead of fearing what I might lose, I began to feel a new sense of freedom. I was looking at life from a place that felt rooted in the center of myself.

There was disruption and upset for my daughter. It helped me to realize that I was acting with a sense of integrity with myself. What kind of example would I have shown her had I continued to swallow my own truth? Part of loving her was loving myself. I began to come forward, claiming my relationship with her.

Leaving my marriage meant big financial change and familiar brushes with struggle. Yet I felt a sense of peace in a way that I never had. With a deep breath, I took a corporate job with a regular paycheck, doing something I had never done before, in a technical field that paid well. It was far from my calling, but it brought me the space and the freedom to see what I wanted in my life—to determine the direction that brought my spirit alive.

I continue to see that there is always a next step. There is always a bigger picture. If I hadn't been willing to trust the guidance of my inner voice, I never would have been able to embrace that bigger picture.

Reflection

Is there something in your life that you recognize you need to let go of? What do you need to be able to act?

Do you honor your inner sensing of what feels "right" for you in your life? How does it show up?

Do you live your life from outside-in (the world of opinion) or from the inside-out?[6]

---

6 Laurie Seymour, "Laying Claim to Myself" in *The Wisdom of Midlife Women 2*, edited by Shann Vander Leek, Inspired Women Kindle Series, 2015, loc. 388-442

44

After the Grail

In the Hero's Journey, the hero returns, having gone through trials and tests, with a gift for their world. You may ask, "What is my gift? What have I returned with? What am I to share with the world?"

These are questions that may follow you through life. After each descent into the underworld, each completion of a trial by fire, each return *to life*, there is a time of questioning and integration before acting.

When you've passed the trials and the tests, when you've come through the dark night of the soul, *what then?* What do you do with this holy grail (of self-discovery, or inner peace, or freedom) that you've found?

Metaphorically, the search for the holy grail is the search for Self, for a deeper, conscious connection with the truth of who you are.

Finding the grail is finally coming home to yourself.

Sometimes, when you've been carrying a heavy sword for a long time, your inner body sensing has no memory of something different to trust. Of what to do next. Or of how life *could* be.

Of what is possible.

Eventually, you begin to wonder whether what you've come through, and who you are now—what you've learned and discovered—could be for more than just you. Maybe it could be a message for your community. *A message that could make a difference in the world.*

These are not things that you question when you are deep inside the belly of the beast. There, your senses are attuned to putting one foot in front of the other, of safely navigating the minefields (do you r*emember how that was?*). You simply want to get through one more day, hoping that tomorrow will somehow be different.

And when you've made it through, *there is relief.* Oh yes, even tears of release from all that you've had to carry. But you're probably feeling a little lost, too, amidst that relief.

Because this is when the questions arrive.

As your feet start to trust the firmness of the ground beneath you, your vision shifts from your inner landscape to the glow of the outer dawning light...and the light you see shining in another's eyes.

Only now do you feel the space to begin to know the deeper story of your journey. In sharing your story, the transformative essence, the *gift of the grail* illuminates your cells. It settles in your body so that your expression of who you are in the world takes on new luminosity.

The gift, the learning, the magic elixir, the holy grail: they are the golden ore that has been mined in your subterranean journey. The story becomes the decoding of your journey through the belly of the beast. It becomes the message, both for you and for the world.

What is *your* vision of what is possible? My own hero's journey has been forgetting that I was loved, of feeling separate, of suffering with that separation. The search became for who I *really* am, for what was true about life.

The search was really to remember. But I didn't know this was what it was until I did, indeed, remember.

I *know* that we are loved. That we are not separate. That we are part of the energetic vastness of the Universe. *I know* that each of us is here to remember that.

The archetypal Hero's Journey, underpinning all versions of the myth, is the journey from forgetting to Remembrance.

This is what is possible.

Dawn's Journey into the Unknown

I shared earlier that it was my experience with Dawn that allowed me to remember the reality of Unconditional Love. These experiences were *initiations*, energetic activations that opened dormant energy systems within me, to catalyze Remembrance of the truth of myself and of life itself.

What I have not shared was how central a role Dawn played in my life, and I in hers. I ran her business for many years, organizing her classes, working with participants outside of class, interfacing with venues, paying bills, and connecting with people around the world. So much of what I know about hosting events, creating beautiful spaces, and planning dinner parties for large groups comes from my years with her.

I might not have my daughter were it not for Dawn. I was married for thirteen years before I got pregnant. Dawn created the space for me to conceive at The Baca Grande, at the end of one of her seminars in 1989.

I was going to leave The Baca as soon as the class ended, going with Dawn and my friend Jane for an adventure in Denver, while Sid stayed behind. Unbeknownst to me, Dawn had received guidance that I needed to stay at The Baca. So, she told me that she needed to spend personal time with Jane for some inner work. Much later, I found out that she told me that, only so I would remain behind and receive what she was told would be available to me at The Baca. We had tried to have a child for a long time, but this time was different. Both Sid and I felt open and expanded, our hearts resonant with one another. There were energies of creation aligning...

The second part of this story is about how she helped me keep my pregnancy.

There were four of us, including Dawn, who were to go to Australia. Dawn's mother (in Canada) was in the process of dying. I was in my first trimester of pregnancy. Nevertheless, we made the trip simply because, as part of the bigger picture, this is what we were to do. We listened to the inner guidance.

It was difficult for Dawn to leave her mother. Yet because her way was to listen, discern, and follow through, we went. Much later I found out that Dawn had been given guidance that we needed to do the trip together so that she could focus energy on me to keep my pregnancy intact.

Energetically (and often physically), Dawn was with me throughout my pregnancy. She taught me ways to move my body to allow more flow, she helped me bring through what supplements to take, how to optimize their use, and how to use toning with my voice to raise the frequency in my cells. Perhaps most importantly, she encouraged a process of inner communication with my unborn daughter. I came to understand what is meant by co-creation in this nine-month communication with my unborn child.

And I understood how the child, this embodying soul developing in the womb, only knows that it is of Source. There is no forgetting, and no separation.

How did Dawn come to this place of being the Initiator?

This is her story in her own words and previously published on the Turaya website.

As a child, I was presented with so much phenomena that no teacher or parent could make me believe that these were dreams, for I knew that I was wide awake when I saw these forms in light. My first experience was during a childhood disease when I was six: scarlet fever. Everyone was concerned about my well-being, but I was as happy as could be living in a loving environment of light forms. I yearned for this experience for years. I grew up in a Christian (Protestant) home. At twelve, I had an electrifying experience in a French Catholic Church, when the Mass was still being celebrated in Latin. At that time, I didn't understand anything from a language place, but I felt an energy that was so powerful that it caused my little body to shake from head to toe. I later converted to Catholicism because of this, but I found that the rite of the Mass had lost its magic for me when celebrated in English.

In my twenties—during the sixties—I became part of that strong inner search that was being experienced by the youth at that time. I traveled to India and throughout the Middle East, spending a lot of time in Egypt. I began to feel a new presence within me, a sense of truth. In Canada, I met a Buddhist monk who had come to North America to teach meditation. I spent the next eighteen years studying with him, learning more and more about this life force which I call energy.

In 1984, I was initiated as a Reiki Master by Phyllis Furumoto into the lineage of Dr. Mikao Usui, a Christian educator in Japan, who had spent his life researching himself and the teachings of Jesus so that he could realize the power of healing within his physical body and share that with his students. In his personal research, he came to full realization of the truth of this. He was given energy symbols that have been transmitted through the lineage in initiation to bring forth the healing power in the initiate so that it can flow from them to others who wish to be healed. As people are healed, they come to a realization of Self-love.

This experience of Self-love was so great for me that it took me to the next phase of my spiritual journey. Once people are healed and realize the potential of this love within them, they must learn to use this surging energy in a creative way. By this time, I had learned to interpret the messages that moved through my body as waves.

My inner guidance had been telling me to go to Japan for a few years. In 1985, I finally made this long-awaited trip. While in Japan, I learned the truth about initiation, and it changed my life forever.

For the first two weeks, I toured many cities and the countryside with my mate and a Japanese friend. I met wonderful people, and Japan was even more beautiful than I had imagined it to be. While still at home, I had read in a Japanese tourist magazine that foreigners were welcome to meditate in temples on Mount Koya. For two weeks, as I toured with my friends, I would ask at tourist information offices about the temples on Mount Koya. These very polite people would always respond in the same way: "What is the name of the temple you wish to visit?" I did not have a name and would always leave the office feeling let down.

I asked my Japanese friend, Kuni, to assist me, but his response just frustrated me. He thought that I should just relax and enjoy Japan and forget about the temple. Kuni stayed to visit his family in Kobe, and my mate and I returned to Tokyo to say goodbye to friends before flying back to Canada. I decided to stay for another two weeks. I knew I wasn't complete and that perhaps I might still find the temple on Mount Koya.

I stayed with my Japanese friends, Marie and Kyoshi, for a few days before striking out on my own to find my temple. I shared with them that I was trying to find an English friend who lived in Kyoto, but had not been successful. Kyoshi looked at the address and said that it was the mailing code for Tokyo, not Kyoto. In Tokyo, the telephone often remains with the owner of the residence. By that evening, Kyoshi had tracked the telephone number for my English friend, Malcom. Sure enough, he was there and happy to hear from me. He had married a Japanese woman, and they were studying Seiki with a woman they referred to as Senza, which means teacher. Their schedule was very full, and they needed to be available to the teacher at all times; however, Malcolm said that he would ask Senza if they could see me.

The next day I received a telephone call from Malcolm and his wife inviting me to have dinner with them. This was a special invitation as his wife was an outstanding cook. We sat down to this incredible meal shortly after I arrived. I had just enough time to sample everything on my plate before the telephone rang. It was Senza, and she wanted to meet me, and they needed to bring me to her immediately. We literally jumped up from the table, leaving that beautiful dinner, and ran out and hailed a taxi.

They explained to me that this was a big honor, for Senza was very busy and did not see many people socially. During the ride, I learned that they had been studying Seiki for three years with Senza and were devoted to her. They didn't know how much longer they would have to study before they were qualified practitioners. I found this fascinating because of my own experience of Reiki. The practice of Seiki seemed similar to Reiki, but there was no initiation involved. That was the reason it took so many years of practice before becoming a qualified practitioner.

Senza's house was big by Japanese standards. We went into a reception room to wait for Senza. She was a large woman with presence. She didn't speak English, but it was obvious through her mannerisms that she wanted to offer me her kind hospitality. Malcolm's wife was our translator. Senza noted that I was not in very good shape. I had traveled in Thailand before coming to Japan, so I was exhausted from my trip. She called a disciple who had been with her for eighteen years and asked him to work on my back. I was amazed. His hand was like my own hand. I knew exactly what he was doing because I had learned to work like this before I was initiated into Reiki. I also had studied meditation and various other energy practices for eighteen years.

Senza sensed my interest and asked her disciple to take me upstairs and prepare me, for she wished to give me a treatment.

Upstairs, I changed into a kimono and lay down on a cot. Senza came and worked on my head while the disciple held my feet. I could feel the energy surging through me. It was so welcome, but not unfamiliar.

We all returned to the room where we were first received, and Senza ordered tea. This all seemed very strange, for I had been told in the taxi that Senza could only spend a few minutes with us because of her very tight schedule. She must have cancelled all of her appointments because we stayed on to discuss Seiki.

Senza was a woman around sixty-five years old and had been practicing Seiki since she was fifteen. If I remember correctly, it seems that her aunt had been initiated in Kyoto and had come home and showed her fifteen-year-old niece the positions. Through the years of focus, Senza had come to understand this form as Seiki. During tea, Senza said if I would stay for two weeks with her, she could give me Seiki. My path had been to go to Mount Koya. Malcolm and his wife were very excited with Senza's offer to me. Senza was very generous and sent us home with her car and driver.

I started to feel this "thing" that I always feel when something is not right for me. I appreciated meeting Senza, and I knew that she and her disciples were doing a lot of good, healing many people in Tokyo and from all over the world, but I still had to deal with the tug of war that was going on within me.

By the time that I returned to Marie and Kyoshi's, they were already asleep. I couldn't sleep. I had to meditate and find out what was happening within me. As the evening's happenings began to replay, I realized that I had never respected Reiki or initiation. I knew a lot about energy when I was initiated into the first level of Reiki. What I had never thought about were the years and years of discomfort I went through in order to experience the energy in the way that I did. Those were my years of healing. In a moment, in that room in my friends' house in Tokyo, I realized the importance of initiation. I could now appreciate that people could experience the energy moving through them immediately after the initiation. There was no need to focus for years and years. I knew that my way had brought me to my inner teacher and the inner voice, but in today's world, very few people have the patience to follow this inner discipline.

I could feel myself filling up with such joy and love as I learned the truth about initiation. I could see that initiation accelerated the process in an incredible way.

It was easy for me to call my friends and give them a message for Senza. I was very grateful for my time with Senza. Perhaps it would have taken me years to come to the truth about initiation if I had not been introduced to Senza and her disciple.

Time out for meditation was more important than ever with this new understanding and appreciation of my own life. I needed to go to Mount Koya.

The next morning, I went to the train station and asked for a ticket to Mount Koya. The man did not speak English and asked, "Koyasan?" I answered "yes" in Japanese thinking he was saying Mount Koya. He wrote my itinerary out on a long piece of paper in Japanese. These directions were very important for I needed to change trains a few times. Each time I would show my itinerary to a train employee, and he would point me or take me to the next train. On the last leg of my journey, I showed my itinerary to a fellow traveler who said in perfect English that he was taking that particular train and invited me to sit with him. I was delighted to have a conversation with someone from that area. He asked me why I was going to Koyasan. I told him about the story that I had read about temples on Mount Koya. He was absolutely shocked that I didn't know where I was going. He told me that Koyasan is a holy city with many temples, but that I wouldn't be able to go there alone. I would have to go with a tour, and then I would only be allowed to stay overnight. He was getting off the train a few stops before Koyasan but invited me to come back to stay with him and his wife. They were language teachers, and he was a Lutheran missionary. His offer was very kind, but I was determined to go to Koyasan.

By the time I got to the end of the line, it had started to rain—torrential rain, and my raincoat was at the bottom of my suitcase. I ran after the other people who had been on the train because this was where we took the cable car to Koyasan. Since I had no idea where I was going, I couldn't lose sight of these people. By the time I got to the cable car, they had already climbed to the top. The conductor indicated that I should get on, so I was on the bottom level looking up at the others. It was pitch black outside and still raining. I could feel the movement of the cable car climbing and my heart was pounding. No one in the world knew where I was, not even me.

At the top of the mountain, everyone seemed to vanish into the mist. I went into a small station where a few men were working at desks. With the help of my dictionary, I was able to make them understand that I wanted to eat and sleep in a temple for ten days. They all laughed heartily and showed me to a stove where I could dry my dress that was soaked from the heavy rain. They were all quite busy making telephone calls to temples on my behalf, but once again, I didn't know because I didn't speak Japanese. An hour is an eternity when you have no idea where or when the next event is going to unfold, when suddenly I was beckoned to the telephone. The voice at the other end of the line said "yes" in English. I was very eager to jump into my story when I was interrupted with these words, "Come to my temple," and she hung up. I went to the desk and once again, with the assistance of my dictionary, I asked for a taxi. And once again, they responded with outrageous laughter. I went back to my cozy spot by the fire to wait for whatever was to happen next. I was in God's hands, and I was near the holy city of Koyasan, so things were working out quite well. I could hardly contain my inner excitement.

A car arrived, and the men who had been working in the station grabbed my bags and showed me outside to a waiting station wagon. I got into the back seat, and we took off at great speed. If I had not been so trusting of my process, I could have been scared, for the driver was quite short. From where I was sitting in the back seat, I couldn't see him, but I could see his eyes in the mirror as they avoided mine. After many hair-raising turns, we entered Koyasan. I couldn't see much except the occasional outline of a temple. I learned later the only reason that I was invited to stay was because I was on the last cable car of the day, and they didn't know what else to do with me. That particular temple where I was invited to stay was chosen because there was an American monk who spoke English. It was decided only the next day that I would be able to stay for a private retreat.

Koyasan was magical. I was taken into many different dimensions where I received my first symbols in Light. I tried to think of Reiki and Dr. Usui, but everything in the past seemed so far away. My inner teacher became so much stronger and more intimate. All that seemed important now was to forget the old and get on with that which was new.

I had no idea just how much had changed until I did my first (Reiki) class in Ottawa in the autumn of 1985. During my talk about Dr. Usui, I began to hear my inner voice like a chant, saying "forget the old and get on with the new." In that moment I could not remember anything about Dr. Usui. I was guided to proceed with the initiations. The organizer became very upset because eighty-five people were there to hear this story. I told her that I had to begin the initiations. I went to the back of the room to wait for the room to empty. I could not imagine anyone wanting to stay to be initiated for I had not told them anything about Reiki. I was feeling absolutely no self-worth when the organizer approached me again and asked why I wasn't beginning. All of the people remaining in the room wanted to be initiated. A class of twenty was considered to be a large class, but fifty-two people—how would I do it? All I could hear from inside was one word, "Proceed."

I took three people behind the partition at a time to initiate them. As I began, the most upsetting experience that I ever had began to happen. Every detail of the Reiki initiation was removed from my consciousness. The inner voice was saying, "Proceed, forget the old, get on with the new." The new symbols were flashing before me in Light, and I was guided with great detail through the new initiation.

I still had questions. Was I doing the right thing by using the new symbols? Were people receiving what they needed to receive or was I ripping them off? Disturbing questions.

After the initiations, it is customary for people to share their experiences. My mind could rest, and my questions were answered because the sharing of experiences had never been so rich. It was apparent that the energy of these symbols connected with people's hearts in a very different way. They were sharing about love, relationships, creativity, and no talk about disease or illnesses. There was a woman in the class whose fingers had been crippled by arthritis. By the end of the class, the pain had disappeared and, I learned later, never returned. What I understood from this was that there seemed to be a healing aspect to this new initiation, but it surely wasn't the focus. The focus was on the feeling of the vibration of love in the physical body. I felt that the people were feeling negative patterns shifting to positive ones very quickly. It was as though this energy was dissolving negativity. This was a quantum change in my work, and I knew that I could trust all that I was hearing and feeling. The love that I felt for my Inner Teacher, the Presence within me that gives me life, was all consuming.

Nothing in my life was more important.

I received guidance to take a group of people to Mexico. I remember announcing this to a group in Ottawa in November of 1985. A man who was at this talk offered to organize the event. It was during this time that I learned about Halley's Comet. In March 1986, about forty of us found ourselves high in the mountains of Mexico at a monastery that was situated between two volcanoes. Each morning at about 3:45 a.m., another colleague and I would climb up the mountain to a level area where there was a soccer field. I would be guided to do certain energy work in the field before the others arrived around 4 a.m. We would all lie down around a large circle in the center of the field, our heads to the outside and feet pointing towards the center.

What an experience! As the comet came into view the temperature would drop at least 30-40 degrees. It was a shock to our systems on the first day. On subsequent days, we came prepared with blankets. As soon as the comet passed out of sight, the balmy Mexico temperature returned.

During this time, there were amazing changes in everyone. I knew that my life had changed as well. I continued to do a few more seminars, but a group was brought together in 1987 that I was to do research with—for how long nobody knew, but everyone bonded together for the purpose of learning from their inner teacher.

The inner law unfolded and became the all-important aspect to embrace. Each person had to learn how to live by his/her inner guidance. It was essential to give up all judgment and to understand Unconditional Love as a high vibration. This vibration of love is what fuels our creativity. All of what I was learning and sharing with this group of people wouldn't mean anything unless it changed their patterns from negative to positive and that they manifested this in their physical lives. They found as a group that there was little or no sickness. They learned that they created everything and that they needed to be responsible for everything that they created, whether it was negative or positive.

Learning to be aligned with the inner teacher was both exciting and joyful. They learned that any discomfort represented imbalance and knew that all they had to do was align themselves so that they could once again experience life flowing and working.

After many years of clearing their own bodies of negative patterns and delving into the deepest part of themselves to know more about truth, they are ready to share themselves as teachers.[7]

So much continued to unfold from this.

One aspect of the mutual mirroring of Dawn's face and my own during my original Initiation with her came about when she brought through this energetic teaching that became Turaya. There were people chosen to receive initiations, some who were chosen to be Turaya Touch© teachers, others as Turaya Meditation© teachers.

Lana and I were to be initiated as Turaya Grand Masters. I was the one to bring this into the world: to speak and to teach. Lana, who had known Dawn since she was very young, held the frequency of Unconditional Love in her cells. If I ever forgot, I knew that she would not.

In our being initiated as Grand Masters, Dawn had the space to continue her own journey, and to focus on the Turaya teachers and the others involved in the original core group of Inner Researchers. We opened the first Turaya Center in Denver, Colorado.

---

7 Dawn Taylor, Turaya.com, 2000, site no longer available

Turaya and the Power of Initiation

Turaya Meditation© and Turaya Touch© came into being through Dawn. They are an expression of her decades of listening to her inner truth and of her openness to receiving new energy systems.

These two forms are different expressions of the same essence.

Some people like to have the more intimate experience of touch. Others prefer the opportunity of silent meditation.

Turaya Meditation© is a process that allows you to connect with your whole being so that more of your creative potential and deeper truth can be revealed to you. During meditation, energy transmissions are made available to you through the use of higher consciousness energy symbols and energy transmissions. This accelerates your ability to enter a deeper level of relaxation and stillness more easily. *And* it opens and deepens your connection with your Creative Intelligence so that it becomes available to you moment to moment throughout your life.

Turaya Meditation© takes you beyond learning how to relax and quiet your thoughts. It is an all-encompassing process that allows you to connect with what I call your *feeling body*. That is the first step in connecting more deeply with your own inner guidance. It opens you to the vast potential that lies within. Then, as you begin to feel an expansion in your heart center, you know that this is what is meant by Unconditional Love. This is the love that fuels your creativity and keeps you healthy.

Turaya Meditation© helps you to make changes in your life, so that you can claim more of your potential. You express new creativity in every area of your life: your work, your health, and your relationships.

Turaya Meditation© accelerates the opening of new dimensions of your awareness. It's like stepping into an ever-changing landscape that offers new possibilities for you to claim at every turn.

Turaya Touch© is a hands-on energy system that works at the cellular level. It helps you go beyond nonproductive patterns—physical, emotional, and mental—so that you can know the truth in your own heart. As you allow this strength to anchor within you, you end cycles of struggle.

As you feel your body sink into a deeply relaxed state, energy blockages are cleared, allowing you to feel a profound sense of nurturing. You begin to appreciate the freedom in surrendering to the strength that is within you. This is what assists you in realizing more of your creative expression, often coming in the form of new insights into yourself as well as into others.

Turaya Touch© reconnects you with your inner wisdom. This integral part of you guides you from moment to moment, with Unconditional Love, throughout your life.

Both Turaya Meditation© and Turaya Touch© help you cross the threshold to remember the truth of your original connection. The foundation of the Turaya Meditation© Intensive classes and the Turaya Touch© Training is the transmission of energy through Initiations. These Initiations allow you to get in touch with that part of you that was never born and will never die. It facilitates your *remembering.*

"The blueprint for conscious evolution is in the cell. But how do you connect with this grand plan?" Dawn Taylor

Everything—your potential, your guidance system, your cellular memory—is already in place within your physical body as an energetic blueprint. It simply needs to be awakened so that you can experience a deeper sense of clarity and inner direction and attract more of what is yours to receive.

Physical life clouds your connection. You get busy, and then you get busier. But one day you wake up in the morning, take a breath, and begin to *awaken*.

Turaya is the fastest way that I know to remember, recover, and come back to the truth of who you are, because it goes beyond any concepts you may have to uplevel the frequency in your cells. You remember your true Self.

It's the Self you have been forever.

The act of remembering becomes a sacred journey. This is the journey that is facilitated by Turaya. Turaya takes you deep within the inner silence—to the mysteries within you, to the alive Remembrance of your original blessing.

This blessing is your connection with Source, with the Creative Intelligence of the Universe. When you receive the Turaya Initiations, you are aligned with your birthright: *to be a creator with the Higher Intelligence that belongs to you.*

Your Creative Intelligence is your connection with the energetic quantum field. It is the way this field expresses through you—your unique expression of God in the physical, 3D world.

The frequencies that are available with Turaya are always new. They reflect the ever-evolving nature of life's journey. As your consciousness evolves, so, too, does your capacity to receive ever-more refined frequencies.

As Carol, who has experienced both Turaya Touch© and Turaya Meditation©, so eloquently put it, "Quite simply, Turaya has changed my life. Healthy in body, yet ailing in spirit, I came to Turaya seeking help. I have been changing and evolving ever since. Almost right away my overworked mind began to settle down. I began to let go of rigid goals, to explore the here and now, and to receive with my heart. All of this began to happen quite naturally, without effort. As a performing artist, my creativity has reached new heights, my mind stepping aside, allowing the heart to lead. There is a sense of expanded consciousness. With my individual purposes less defined, I feel much more open to the bigness of life."

Your Quantum Connection

"A quantum leap is the unexpected that comes to you with sudden grace... A quantum leap, by definition, means moving into uncharted territory with no guide to follow."

-Price Pritchett, Ph.D., *you²*

Staying inside the confines of the proverbial box, (the boundaries you adopt through the way you have been educated, raised, and through your belief systems, habits, and way of being) inhibits your ability to make a quantum leap. By their nature, quantum leaps are unscripted, with the landing point (the other side of the leap) often far beyond the dimensions of said box. Which means that you need to be aware that your beliefs are just that—beliefs, and not necessarily the final word.

You also need a willingness to explore your beliefs. And also, a willingness to set them aside for a while to explore possibilities *beyond what you already know.*

That last part is key. There is a whole universe beyond and outside of what you know. The journey is to allow more and more of what lies outside the realm that you consider *you* to be brought into your sphere of Self. *Herein lies your potential.* Believe it or not, it is also your genius. Genius is far more than what you are good at. That's only the beginning. If you are here to bring something new into being, then you must cross into the territory marked "unknown." This is where you tap into your greater potential. Remember that you are completely and utterly unlike everyone else.

There is a reason you are here, that you came into this world at this time. It doesn't mean that there is an overarching goal you must have.

It means that *you* are vital to the whole. And that is both simply and magnificently *the truth*. This is the realm of your genius.

Without your unique expression, without your particular set of experiences, there would be something missing in the fabric of what lives in the continually evolving universe. This is the energetic blueprint that you arrived with when you were born.

Ultimately, remembering your connection to Source brings you into your genius. It activates this original blueprint of who you are, allowing everything that you embark upon to flow with ease. Because this is what happens when you act in concert with your inner guidance.

I've been reflecting quite a bit these days, looking back on my life as I move forward into what is next. One of the themes that has been emerging is how fear and doubt show up when making massive changes. Even after all these years of "embracing the unknown," this still happens for me. It seems that as I make even bigger changes, there is still the familiar duo of fear and doubt that make an appearance.

Of course, every change comes packaged in the unknown. What will happen? What if I don't do it? Can I really do this? How will it work out? Will I be okay? What's the next step? Who will it impact?

Exploring beyond the known, looking to the other side of the horizon, is, by its nature, a step off the cliff.

It always takes courage and some amount of trust to step out. To know that you will, in fact, be okay. Maybe even better than okay: you can *thrive*.

The magic comes for me when I feel that alchemical blend of courage and trust. It happens when I've allowed a new frequency to be activated in me. Even though it is unfamiliar, I recognize that it is asking me to surrender *into* it.

What is most useful when stepping into the unknown? At the same time that I remember how often I've been here— how familiar this fear and doubt are that have surfaced—I also know that I must enter the *void* with nothing in my hands. No expectations, no plan, no judgment. The void is open space. It contains *nothing* and *everything* at once. It is unknown, and therefore, there are no markers to bring familiarity and comfort.

Your tendency may be to explain away this feeling of the void. To fill the void with what you *think* is happening.

But what you *think* can only be based on what you already know. And if you are moving beyond that, you must learn to become at least a little bit comfortable hanging out in the unknown. In the space between what has ended and before something new unfolds.

Open hands and a willing heart allow you to actively receive what becomes available when you cross the threshold. It's the next step of the Hero's Journey.

This is where your potential—your genius—lies. If you have dreamed it, it's because the blueprint is already there within you, just waiting to be activated as you remember.

Evolution or Quantum Leap: How to Understand Your Changes

After you surrender to receive, after the space of the void, there comes the urge to move forward.

Right now, the speed of change is breathtaking. Barely do you recognize the new landscape that has dropped into view when you are whisked onto the next.

Sometimes you experience a multiplicity of dimensions simultaneously. It feels as if you cannot get a firm grasp on who you are.

And sometimes you time-shift, moving so rapidly between dimensions that it *feels* as if you were in multiple times at once.

In between the changes, you experience the silent pause of the void—the space between what was and what will be. It is the space between the in-breath and the out-breath.

Ever felt this way? It's unsettling!

In fact, you are being asked to lay claim to a bigger and bigger picture of what is possible. This disquieting energy is the means to the quantum leap. It's upending life as you've known it. It's what you've asked for over and over from the Universe. *Most importantly, you are being given what is needed.*

Then you must integrate it into your understanding and into your life, so that you can allow what is possible.

You may be wondering how to make this quantum leap. Because you *want* to reveal and receive what is available so that you can manifest it.

Alignment is essential. Where to begin?

Sometimes you may notice your changes as new awareness. Awareness initiates cellular transformation. Then your physical body needs to catch up with what the consciousness is experiencing. Your body needs to align with the new dimensions of consciousness that have been tapped.

I call this part of the process the *decoding* of the experience.

Sometimes the cellular change is triggered first, whether by direct energetic application (as in energy work like Turaya Touch© or through an Initiation) or by the impact of unseen forces (as in the cosmic vibrational waves that frequently affect the planet).

The body remembers, too. As your body receives and incorporates new energy systems, your consciousness itself plays a kind of catch-up. New energetic systems are activated and experienced as remembering.

And truly, it is not one and then the other. That's just your linear self, wanting to make sense of it all.

Realize that as you raise your vibratory rate, there is more and more light that is integrating into your cellular structure *and* in your consciousness. You experience this through your individual blueprint.

You came into this physical world with your connection with Source intact, and now you reclaim the inheritance that is yours.

As you lay claim to a new energetic lineage that transcends your historical roots, you receive your inheritance. It is part of the promise that was made in being born. This is a moment of profound significance for your well-being.

You are enabled to act with recognition of all that you have been gifted. Your potential is activated.

As humans, at any time, we live with partial awareness. Awareness is like the moon, though. Even though you only see a portion of what exists, you *know* there is more. You have a Remembrance of *more*. This carries you ever forward, discovering what feels to be new, watching intently for what is revealed.

How do you receive that? What are you to do with it?

This, too, is part of the decoding process.

You imagine there must be a purpose. What could this be? Is it something unique to you or is it a collective purpose?

It is indeed both. It is up to you to take your individual and unique place with these energies. When you align with these energies, you can determine, moment by moment, the direction in which you are to next place your feet. Only then can the collective purpose be realized.

It is with this experience of energy that decoding is needed. Energy is received by the body via the cells. It must then be converted into "language" that is intelligible: consciousness. You cannot sustain the level of transformation that is the quantum leap without the corollary opening of conscious understanding. Your system (you) requires it so that you can integrate these energetic changes. Which then becomes the raw material with which you craft your life.

So it is that Inner Research becomes an indispensable element of conscious evolution. Through asking questions and allowing yourself to receive the inner answers, consciousness is revealed. Pay attention to what feels new in your everyday life. Notice new ways of thinking and being. Be aware of fresh ideas and pictures that spring to mind.

This is the path of integration necessary for transformation: in the cell, in consciousness, in relationships, and in social structures. In the world.

It is magnificent.

Change in Everyday Life

I had dinner recently with two dear friends who were part of the original group of researchers with Dawn. As our conversation deepened, I was aware of how seen and acknowledged I felt, and how easy it was for me to experience them as who they are *now*. Not last month or last week, *now* embraces all that has opened and evolved into the present moment. It was delicious and inspiring.

Sometimes, we are moved on from existing relationships or friendships. Someone has been a friend for years, and yet, you are no longer drawn to be with them.

It's human nature to "fix" our loved ones into the way in which we know them, not accounting for their personal evolution and growth. What happens? We see them through old lenses that aren't flexible enough to be with them as they are now. Familiarity breeds continuing familiarity, only in this case, it's no longer true.

We must continually update our own operating system in order to be on the expansion trajectory that is available to us. But when those around us are only able to see the "old" us, something feels off. They are clinging to who we used to be so that they don't feel threatened. "If you change you might leave me." "You've changed!" they say accusingly.

Yes, of course, I have. Isn't that why we are here? To grow, to learn, to discover?

If we aren't aware of what is happening, we will try and fit back into that old skin, already discarded and no longer functional, so as not to disturb the status quo. But when we are aware, we get to be who we are, even when that means something changes in the relationship. It's not that we don't care. It's just that the status quo no longer exists.

It may take years to recognize this for what it is so that we can step away without blaming anyone involved. When you hear someone say that they've outgrown their mate, it's most likely because neither one is able to recognize the new person before them. When you open yourself to discover who your mate is today, you, too will be changed, igniting new creativity and passion in the discovery. This is how the relationship transforms and evolves.

Quite a while back, I realized the impact of change both in how I am inside and how I show up in the world. In order to track and be curious about my day-to-day changes, I pay attention to how others respond to me.

With old friends, there is a feeling of comfort, yes, but sometimes also limitation. If they cannot see my changes, they don't update their interactions with me, endeavoring (even in the kindest way) to relate in the comfort of what is known.

I don't diminish these relationships with old friends. Nor with my mate. They are precious. We also need those around us who haven't known us before. They are better able to see us as we are now, which energetically supports our continuing expansion as well as the discovery of who we are NOW.

50

A Vision for the World

Love has no need to conquer anything. Love simply invites you to remember your original connection. When it permeates your cells, old patterns dissolve. Self-doubt and fear fall to inner knowing. To trust.

This is not the end of the story. What then becomes possible? In order to sustain your health and well-being, it is essential that you utilize the creative life force for expression in the world. The life force is a *creative* force, always, as Jennifer Hough, author of *Unstuck*, puts it, "creating upon creation."

What is self-expression, then, if not the expression of Self, that which is the interface of the personal *you* with Source?

- What if you knew your life had purpose and meaning and direction? Creative Intelligence, when expressed from Remembrance of your connection with this force, holds all of these.
- What if each person you were in a relationship with knew that you both are *already* loved? Then there is no need to compare, to manipulate, to have power over, or to protect yourself from fear of being hurt.
- What if, in business, you and each member of your team have this kind of knowing? What could you create together? What problems could be solved? True innovation would not be simply an iteration of what already exists.

The intensity of what we witness in our world today: political divides, wars on multiple fronts, personal isolation, countless judgments of us vs. them—all have within them an aspect of separation from Source, of forgetting who we truly are.

The answer lies in recognizing that God is alive and well within every single one of us.

We must remember.

This is what I invite you to step into. Cross the threshold to all that lies within you, waiting, ready for you to remember.

What We Are Called to Now

There is a bigger picture still.

People are feeling more isolated than ever. Our muscles of personal engagement with others have atrophied. It's not enough to remember your own original connection. A rebuilding of the community is needed.

It is key to co-creating what you are here to do in the world. *Oneness contains our relationship with one another.*

For some time now, my inner guidance has been showing me pictures of small gatherings in different locations around the world, called *Salons of Life*. Hosts invite their friends to come together in an intimate, comfortable space where the energies of connection and Remembrance are activated.

The Salons are weaving the sacred connection of global Remembrance. This grows the connective tissue of you with others on this path of Remembrance.

For more information on how to host a Salon in your city, or to be included in one where you live, visit

www.thebacainstitute/Salons

For You Who Illuminate the Way

Have you noticed that giving and receiving is one dynamic? Each is embedded in the other. A metaphorical energetic quantum entanglement. It is the essence of circulation.

There are days where your focus is directed on accomplishing the tasks on your list. Meetings, news of the day, errands, traffic, others' needs, deadlines, social media: they grab hold of your awareness.

In a moment, you've forgotten who you *really* are.

In the same way, you get derailed by your own thoughts: self-doubt, fear, anxiety, indecision. You know that this is simply another moment of forgetting.

Moments connect in a stream that become patterns. But patterns are just that: patterns. Nothing more. Patterns of behavior, patterns of thought. They are not the truth. You do not need to believe in them.

Instead, look for the light and turn inside. Yes, inside, in the quiet. There, the light lives, steady, constant, ready to illuminate your journey.

Let yourself be drawn inside.

Look deeper than your patterns. There is more. Have you noticed that your inner light grows brighter as you give it your attention?

The light is embedded in your cells. It's part of your DNA. This light nourishes you, reminding you of the bigger picture whenever you forget.

The inner light never dims. As you turn your focus to the light, it becomes brighter still, as if fed by your gaze.

What is needed? Your attention. Not the attention of critical analysis, but the soft focus of acknowledgment and receiving.

An Invocation and Remembrance

> You are here within me. You are everywhere, so I have no need to look outside myself to find you. I only need turn inward and receive, for you are the light of my life and I am forever grateful for your Presence.

Some moments you may feel tired. The picture keeps growing of what is to unfold from your actions. You don't have to know how this will happen. You don't have to know how to contain it all.

Remember that you are nothing by yourself. You are in partnership with Presence, and your partner knows infinitely more than you. You have been given the picture. Your part is to remain constant with it. To act with the right timing. To listen, growing the light within you so that it illuminates your way. Then, perhaps, it can illuminate the way for someone else, too.

Isn't this what you want in your life? To expand your light and shine the way?

Continue to practice with your breath. Notice the sensations when you consciously breathe in. Receive your breath with a feeling of gratitude. Your breath keeps you alive. It connects you with every living thing.

What do you receive in your life? What is your list?

My own picture that was given to me? A community of those committed to their own journey of discovery—of remembering the truth. You become part of this community, if you choose, simply in your desire to receive and to remember.

Open your heart, your mind, your hands. Do it in each moment. Do it with love. Receive yourself first. This makes it possible to remember and then to come together with others as one—*oneness with the many.*

In the quiet. It all begins here. Receive, receive, receive.

You are already luminous. Allow your light to expand, to illuminate the way for another.

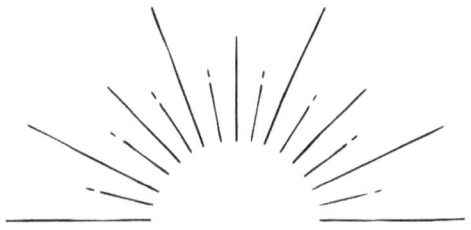

CODA

I wrote these words many years ago: "The power of realizing your own story connects you with your purpose."

Having written this book, I have, of course, written my own story. Yet, like the myth of the hero, I have also written it as much for you as for myself. I have been through trials. I have been initiated. I have received knowledge. And I have spent decades teaching, counseling, and mentoring others. Now I am bringing what I have remembered to a wider stage to shine light where it is needed. To allow *you* to look into your own mirror and to claim the truth for yourself. To be a master of yourself.

This is my purpose. In this moment.

This is the only way that it can be.

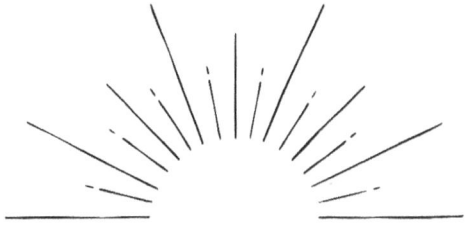

Resources for Continued Exploration

1. Quantum Connection Quiz: What's Your Quantum Connection Archetype?

2. The Baca Institute Programs: Turaya Touch© Training; Turaya Meditation Live Online©; Inner Guidance Mastery Blueprint; Inspiration into Action; Quantum Co-Creation; Mastery Program (Contact Laurie for more information)

3. Wisdom Talk Radio: Laurie's podcast explores conscious living, including energy, education, relationships, creativity, spirituality, purpose, self-awareness, science, business, and more.

4. Gail Larsen: Real Speaking and Wisdom Talk Radio interview

5. Michael Newton, Ph.D., *Journey of Souls*

6. Simone Wright: *First Intelligence* and Wisdom Talk Radio interview

7. Joseph Campbell: *Hero With a Thousand Faces*; Bill Moyers interview series

8. The Bonny Method of Guided Imagery and Music (GIM)

9. Kathleen McGowan (in-depth research and writing about Mary Magdelene) Wisdom Talk Radio interview

10. Crista Marie Miller (*teachings from Mary Magdalene*)

11. Jennifer Hough: *Unstuck: The Physics of Getting out of Your Own Way* and Wisdom Talk Radio interview

12. Rupert Sheldrake: Wisdom Talk Radio interview

13. Hildegard of Bingen. She was a twelfth-century German abbess, writer, composer, Christian mystic, and theologian. *A Feather on the Breath of God* is a recording of sacred vocal music written by her.

14. Nathalie Coral Lepeltier: Conscious Future Institute and *Quantum Heart: a Guide to Lead From the Future*

15. The Octopus Movement: a global tribe of thinkers, creators and visionaries, creators, and visionaries embracing the beauty of human diversity.

To find these resource links and other bonus material, scan the code below:

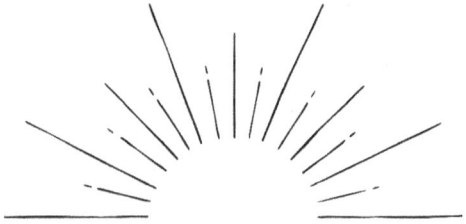

Acknowledgments

With a deep bow of gratitude and acknowledgment, and so much love...

To my writing, publishing, and marketing team:

My editor, Lois Rose: We'll always have Malbrans! Sitting next to each other at your dining room table in your tiny French village, talking through each page: what joy creating together! Thank you for your sustained belief in my ideas and for helping me refine this book with your unfailing patience, dedication, and love. This book would not be what it is without you.

Kathy Sparrow: Thank you for your guidance on my publishing journey. You always have an answer to my array of questions! I so appreciate your loving support.

Donna Cravotta: Your contributions have been invaluable for this final creation and how it is making its way into the world. You brought magic! Thank you!

Crista Marie Miller: Thank you for your guidance and support in birthing this book. You brought so much in your message from Dawn!

Suzanne Dudley-Schon: my first reader and visionary editor! Thank you for your feedback that helped me with both the acknowledgment of what I was trying to craft and input that helped steer my course.

Sabrina Fritts, you opened the first door for me to write this book. Thank you!

Annet Hoeijmans-Boon, whose intuitive flow painting became the cover. Thank you for this extraordinary gift from your creative heart.

Cathi Stevenson from Book Cover Express for transforming a painting into a book cover. Gwen Gades from Be a Purple Penguin for the interior formatting.

Nancy Swisher: Our conversations about writing so often have stirred me to new understandings. I so appreciate our friendship.

My advance readers, Gail Larsen, Diane Soloman, Pierre Goirand: Your feedback was invaluable to what was born (even when it was hard to hear). Thank you for being in my life.

The Fab 4: Co-creating with you is joyful.

My extended family: Sarah, Leon, Shane, Colm, Carolyn, Vanessa, Edward, Lana. Your love always helps me remember.

Roy: You may not remember the life we have lived together, but you unfailingly meet me with love. I am so grateful.

Dawn, my dear daughter: You are the gift that I continue to discover. My heart is full. (You and Joe do make adorable babies! I didn't know how becoming Bubbie was going to feel. It really is the best thing going.)

Jane: Your all-the-time love continues to sustain me. Thank you for always seeing me for who I am.

Dawn, as I said in the beginning, without you I would never have known that this was my book to write. My heart thanks you daily for my life. I love you.

About the Author

Author photo by Sara Brentano.

Host of the **Wisdom Talk Radio** podcast, Quantum Connection Mentor, international trainer and speaker, and Certified Master Trainer, **Laurie Seymour, M.A.**, is the founder and CEO of **The Baca Institute**. She has dedicated her life to showing how to reliably connect with your energetic Creative Intelligence (Source), dissolving old patterns of difficulty, struggle, and self-sabotage.

Over twenty-five years ago, Laurie was honored to receive the stewardship of a special energetic technology, *Turaya*, that activates your inner connection with Source, raising your vibration (which changes *everything*) and giving you the ability to create through your connection with the infinite quantum field of potential.

After twice leaving successful careers, first as a psycho-therapist and trainer, and then as a solutions engineer in the telecom industry, Laurie founded The Baca Institute, honoring the twenty-five years of Inner Research she and a small group of intrepid explorers did in exploring human potential through activating new energy systems.

Laurie is the creator of the **Quantum Connection Process**, helping you build a program, business, and life that expresses your Divine blueprint, celebrates your Creative Intelligence genius, AND gives you the financial flow you deserve with the time, health and well-being to enjoy it.

Laurie Seymour

While she makes her home in Denver, Colorado, Laurie has a special place in her heart for France. She enjoys exploring cultures through travel, food, language, and music. She also has two grandchildren who bring unending joy to her heart.

Unconditional Remembrance: Your Connection to Source is Laurie's first solo book, and within it, she shares the wisdom of remembering our original connection to love and to our Source. When we do, we can live more creative, meaningful, and abundant lives—on purpose.

Laurie has a master's degree from Cold Mountain Institute/ Antioch University, is a Fellow of the Institute for Music and Imagery, and has a Certified Master Trainer certificate from the Evolutionary Business Council.

For more information about Laurie and her work, visit: https://thebacainstitute.com/

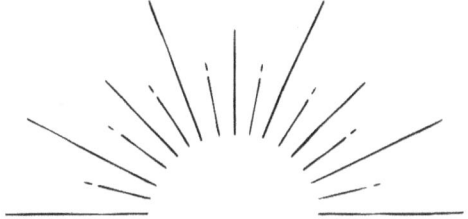

About Scribe Hive Publishing

Scribe Hive Publishing LLC is dedicated to publishing great reads. Learn about our authors, available titles, and more at:

www.scribehivepublishing.com

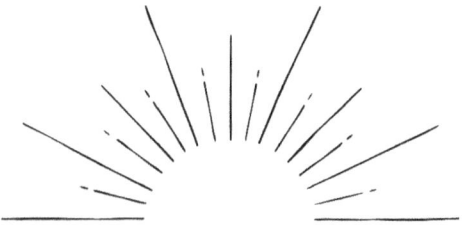

Continue the Journey!

If this book resonated with you, you might be interested in Turaya Meditation© Live Online with Laurie.

Turaya Meditation© allows you to connect with your physical body and your inner self so that more of your creative potential and deeper truth is revealed to you. During the meditation time, energy transmissions are made available through the use of higher consciousness energy symbols. This accelerates you more easily entering a deeper level of relaxation and stillness. It opens and deepens your connection with your creative intelligence.

If you would like to have a Quantum Connection call with Laurie, you can schedule that here: Quantum Connection Exploratory Call (www.thebacainstitute.com/contact/).

You can find more of Laurie's writing at
www.thebacainstitute.com

www.ingramcontent.com/pod-product-compliance
Lightning Source LLC
Chambersburg PA
CBHW051146120626
46547CB00012B/958

9 781962 112277